LANGUAGE IN SOCIETY 10

Dialects in Contact

LANGUAGE IN SOCIETY

GENERAL EDITOR:
Peter Trudgill, Professor of Linguistic Science,
University of Reading

ADVISORY EDITORS:
Ralph Fasold, Professor of Linguistics,
Georgetown University
William Labov, Professor of Linguistics,
University of Pennsylvania

Dialects in Contact

PETER TRUDGILL

First published 1986

Basil Blackwell Ltd
108 Cowley Road, Oxford OX4 1JF, UK

Basil Blackwell Inc.
432 Park Avenue South, Suite 1503,
New York, NY 10016, USA

British Library Cataloguing in Publication Data

Trudgill, Peter
    Dialects in contact.
    1. Dialectology   2. Grammar, Comparative and general
    I. Title
    471'.2   P201

    ISBN 0–631–12691–0
    ISBN 0–631–12733–X Pbk

Library of Congress Cataloging in Publication Data

Trudgill, Peter.
    Dialects in contact.
    (Language in society; 10)
    Bibliography: p.
    Includes index.
    1. English Language—Dialects. 2. English Language—Social aspects.
3. Language in contact. I. Title. II. Series: Language in society (Oxford, Oxfordshire); 10.
PE1711.T7 1986 427 85–30815
ISBN 0–631–12691–0
ISBN 0–631–12733–X (pbk.)

Typeset by Katerprint Co. Ltd, Oxford
Printed in Great Britain by T.J. Press Ltd, Padstow

Contents

Acknowledgements

This book has been a long time coming – too long, I suspect, in the view of the publishers – and has been worked on in many different locations. I am particularly grateful to colleagues and students who discussed topics in the field of dialect contact with me at the Australian National University, the University of Illinois, Stanford University, the University of Texas at Austin, and the University of Toronto, as well as at the University of Reading. I am also especially grateful to Philip Carpenter, J. K. Chambers, Nikolas Coupland, Ralph Fasold, Jean Hannah, John Harris, Richard Hudson, James Milroy, and Lesley Milroy, who read earlier drafts of the book and gave invaluable advice, only some of which fell on deaf ears. I have also, I hope, benefited from discussions with and vital information received from the following, to whom I also express my thanks: Ian Bild, William Downes, Janet Fletcher, Tina Foxcroft, Elizabeth Gordon, Ian Hancock, John Holm, Ernst Håkon Jahr, L. W. Lanham, Tom Melchionne, Helge Omdal, James S. Ryan, Alison Shilling, Gary Underwood, Keith Walters, and Jeffrey P. Williams.

I would like to thank the following for permission to redraw and reproduce figures: Cambridge University Press (1.4, 1.5, 1.6); Professor J. K. Chambers (1.7); Mouton de Gruyter (1.1, 1.2, 1.3). I am also grateful to the following for permission to redraw and reproduce maps: Cambridge University Press (3.15); Croom Helm Ltd (2.9, 2.10); Edward Arnold (4.4); Universiteitsforlaget, Oslo, Norway (3.4).

Introduction

This book is concerned with the subject of linguistic change. It is, however, about only a very restricted set of all the possible types of change that can occur in language. It is concerned, in fact, with those changes that take place during or as a consequence of contacts between closely related varieties of language. It deals with how and why mutually intelligible linguistic varieties may influence one another, as well as with the social and geographical spread of linguistic forms from one dialect to another. It also focuses on the way in which, in certain dialect mixture situations, totally new dialects may be formed. These changes clearly form only a fraction of the changes that can occur in human languages, and I do not wish to overstate the importance of the role of dialect contact in inducing change. Nevertheless, it emerges that a very great deal of information is already available in the literature on particular instances of contact-induced change, and an extensive study of these works does suggest very strongly that dialect contact is, in its way, as important an area for investigation as language contact.

The work is very much a study in sociolinguistics. This is especially so in that it argues for the crucial importance, in the study of dialect contact, of human behaviour in face-to-face interaction. Unlike many interactional sociolinguistic studies, however, it concentrates, in the manner of Labovian-style secular linguistics, on language form rather than on matters of greater concern to social scientists.

What I have tried to do in this book is to examine a number of the particular instances of dialect contact described in the literature, both in my own work and that of others, and draw from them, as far as possible, general conclusions about the forces that appear to be at work during the processes involved in dialect contact. My method has been to attempt explanations – usually very *ad hoc* – for developments that have occurred in one situation, and then to see if these can be generalized to other similar situations.

The ultimate goal of work of this type will be to predict exactly what will occur when one dialect, with a given set of linguistic and demographic characteristics, comes into contact in a particular way with another dialect with different characteristics. Happily, since – as Howard Giles has pointed out – human beings are not sociolinguistic automata, there seems no chance at all of our ever being able to do this with anything approaching total success. Perhaps, however, this book is a small beginning.

1

Accommodation between Dialects

The subject of *languages in contact* was brilliantly investigated by Uriel Weinreich, with particular reference to the bilingual speaker, in his 1953 book of the same name. It has also, of course, been treated subsequently by many other writers. Most of the linguistic processes that take place during language contact, and which have therefore been discussed by Weinreich and these more recent writers, appear to occur in the first instance as a result of individual bilingualism. This form of bilingualism, in its turn, takes place because communication would not be possible without it. If speakers of two mutually unintelligible languages are to communicate through the medium of language, some degree of individual bilingualism is obviously required. The presence, then, of two or more varieties within the repertoires of single speakers leads to influence and interaction, some of it of the type often labelled 'interference'. The languages that are in contact with each other socially may become changed linguistically, as a result of also being in contact psychologically, in the competences of individual speakers.

The present book is similarly interested in the way in which contact may lead to change. However, it deals not with languages but with *dialects in contact*, by which is meant contact between varieties of language that are mutually intelligible at least to some degree. In this type of contact situation, many of the linguistic developments that may take place are not strictly speaking necessary from a purely communicative point of view, although of course comprehension difficulties may occur. Nevertheless, it can readily be observed that related, mutually intelligible dialects do have an effect on one another in contact situations, with or without the development of individual bidialectalism. Very often, for example, when two speakers of different varieties of the same language which are completely mutually intelligible come into contact and converse, items may be transferred from one of the varieties to the other. For instance, if a speaker of American English and a speaker of English English come into contact, each of them knowing very well that, say, American English *sidewalk* corresponds to English English *pavement*, it is perfectly possible that the American will eventually start saying *pavement*, and/or that the English person will begin to say *sidewalk* – even though there is no strictly communicative point in their doing so.

Exactly why this kind of thing should happen is not immediately clear. One theory that seeks to explain these apparently unnecessary linguistic modifications is that developed by the social psychologist Howard Giles. Giles (1973) writes of conversational situations that 'if the sender in a dyadic situation wishes to gain the receiver's approval, then he may adapt his accent patterns towards that of this person, i.e. reduce pronunciation dissimilarities.' Giles labels this process 'accent convergence', and points out that the reverse process, 'accent divergence', may take place instead if, for example, speakers wish to dissociate themselves from or show disapproval of others. These processes of convergence and divergence can clearly also take place at the grammatical and lexical levels (though see Coupland, 1984), and are presumably part of a wider pattern of behaviour modification under the influence of and in response to others. Scholars in fields such as communications and psychology have, indeed, investigated this type of convergence/divergence behaviour with reference to many other non-linguistic factors such as body movement, proximity, speech rhythm, speech speed, silence, gaze direction, eye contact, and so on. (A critical summary is provided by Gatewood and Rosenwein, 1981 in their paper on interactional synchrony. See also Cappella, 1981; Dittman, 1962, 1972; Feldstein, 1972; Jaffe and Feldstein, 1970; Kendon, 1970; and Patterson, 1973, 1983.) There is in this literature a strong sense that convergence of this type is a universal characteristic of human behaviour.

In any case, behavioural convergence is obviously a topic of natural and central interest for social psychologists, and language provides them with a very useful site for the study of this phenomenon. Giles and his co-workers, as social psychologists of language, have developed, using language as data, the theory alluded to above and labelled by them *accommodation theory*. This theory focuses on speech, and discusses and attempts to explain why speakers modify their language in the presence of others in the way and to the extent that they do. It also examines the effects and costs of this type of modification.

Giles's initial (1973) paper looks mainly at convergence and divergence in short-term contacts and in terms of adjustments up and down the social dimension from high-prestige to low-prestige accents. In situations where speakers with accents of different social status come into contact, the direction in which accommodation will take place is often problematical, and Giles and others have devoted considerable attention to exploring what factors are involved in determining who accommodates to who; why speakers do it; to what extent they do it; and how it is perceived by others (see Giles et al., 1973).

From the perspective of the linguist, however, it is clear that accommodation can also take place between accents that differ regionally rather than socially, and that it can occur in the long term as well as in the short term. In long-term contacts, who accommodates to who is less problematical, since, in most cases where this phenomenon can be observed, we are dealing with contact between speakers of different regional varieties, and with regionally mobile individuals or minority groups who accommodate, in the long term, to a non-mobile majority that they have come to live amongst. The problem is then one of determining how speakers accommodate, the extent to which they accommodate, and why some situations and some individuals produce more – or different types of – accommodation than others. Long-term accommodation is therefore of less interest for the social psychologist, but of considerable interest to the linguist.

Short-term accommodation

Work in accommodation theory on short-term accommodation between speakers with socially different accents has proved to be most insightful from a sociopsychological perspective. It has been found, for example, that linguistic convergence in a socially downward direction can lead, in some cultures, to speakers being evaluated as kinder and more trustworthy than if they do not converge (Giles and Smith, 1979); and that, if a person anticipates meeting another 'socially significant' person in the immediate future, then the latter's speech (if, say, overheard) is perceived by the former as being more like the former's own speech than would otherwise be the case. Many other examples could be given.

From a linguistic point of view, however, work on accommodation theory has until recently been less informative. This is not, of course, intended as a criticism of the work of social psychologists, since their objectives were obviously very different. However, it is apparent that many more insights, in addition to those already obtained, could be gained by more linguistically sophisticated analyses of the accommodation process itself than those initially employed by Giles and his associates. In the work of these social psychologists, for instance, the degree of linguistic accommodation indulged in by speakers is measured impressionistically. Typically, tape recordings of speakers are played to groups of linguistically naïve subjects who are asked to assess them in terms of accent 'broadness'. No actual linguistic analysis is involved at all. It is apparent, however, that detailed linguistic analyses of the accommodation process would bring with them a number of benefits for both social psychologists and, especially, linguists. For example they would permit, amongst other things:

(1) An exact, rather than impressionistic, quantification of degree of linguistic accommodation;
(2) An examination of which linguistic features are and are not changed during accommodation, together with explanations for this;
(3) A study of whether accommodation is a uniform process, or whether linguistically different types of accommodation take place in the case of different speakers, different situations, or different relationships;
(4) A study of the limits of accommodation: what are the linguistic (as opposed to social and psychological) constraints on accommodation, and is it possible to accommodate totally to a new variety?

Quantification of accommodation

We begin by dealing with the first of these benefits – that which arises from exact rather than impressionistic quantification. We bear in mind in so doing that it has been one of the achievements of sociolinguistics to demonstrate that the quantification of linguistic phenomena can reveal hitherto unsuspected findings of considerable importance. Given that this is so, we must expect that exact quantification will provide an analysis of the accommodation process more revealing than that of the social psychologist.

We can illustrate this particularly clearly by examining those situations in which social psychologists have been most interested, namely those involving short-term accommodation between speakers with socially different accents. For example, Coupland (1984), in a pioneering study of the linguistic accommodation of an assistant in a travel agency to customers, in Cardiff, Wales, investigates three Cardiff English variables. These are:

(1) /h/ vs. Ø in *house, hammer* etc.
(2) [t] vs. [ḍ] in *better, city* etc.
(3) /ŋ/ vs. /n/ in *walking, waiting* etc.

Figures 1.1, 1.2, and 1.3, from Coupland (1984), show a very clear correlation between the assistant's pronunciation and those of 51 of her clients grouped by social class. In fact, Coupland writes that the percentages of variants in her speech 'prove to be almost as good an indicator of the socioeconomic class and educational background of her interlocutors as the percentage of those forms in the groups of clients' own speech'. Indeed, Coupland's study as a whole is an excellent example of the benefits of quantification in the study of accommodation.

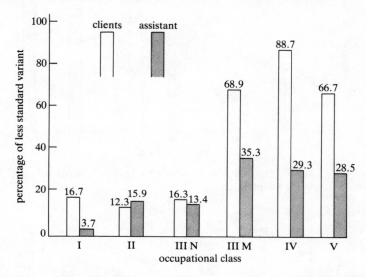

Figure 1.1   Variable (h): comparison of clients' use and assistant's use; clients by occupation (from Coupland, 1984)

A further example of this type of quantification is the following. In his initial paper, Giles (1973) argues that the process of accommodation may lead to circularity in the research of sociolinguists. In a comment on Labov's work in New York City (Labov, 1966), Giles suggests that it may be the case that when they are interviewing informants, sociolinguists expect the pronunciation of their informants to correlate with, say, social class. The interviewing linguist therefore accommodates in anticipation, as it were, and speaks with a 'broader', more regional accent when interviewing lower-class speakers than when recording higher-class informants. The informants in the face-to-face situation then accommodate to the interviewer, producing the sort of language that was expected and fulfilling the sociolinguist's prophecy. The results of some sociolinguistic surveys may therefore, according to Giles, be somewhat suspect.

Most practising sociolinguists would, I believe, wish to reject this hypothesis rather strongly. Certainly my own feeling concerning my

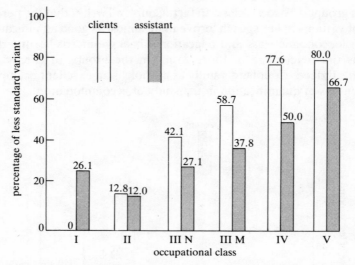

Figure 1.2   Variable (t): comparison of clients' use and assistant's use; clients by occupation (from Coupland, 1984)

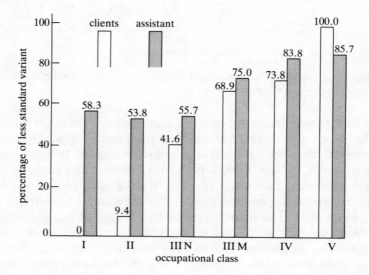

Figure 1.3   Variable (ng): comparison of clients' use and assistant's use; clients by occupation (from Coupland, 1984)

survey of the English spoken in Norwich (Trudgill, 1974) was that accommodation did indeed take place but that I accommodated linguistically to my informants rather than inducing them to accommodate to me. As a native of the area I was investigating, moreover, I had done this easily and in a relatively automatic, subconscious way. (In carrying out linguistic interviews, as is well known, one wants as much as possible to reduce the effect of the 'observer's paradox' (Labov, 1972) and to put informants at their ease. One has to behave, dress and speak in the manner most likely to produce relaxed conversation, and linguistic convergence is part of this overall pattern.) I had, however, no direct evidence to support this feeling, or to refute Giles's hypothesis. What was required was a quantitative study of the accommodation process as it had occurred during my sociolinguistic interviews.

To investigate the extent to which accommodation occurred, I therefore began an analysis of my own speech as an interviewer on my Norwich tape recordings. Linguistic self-analysis by interviewers has been carried out before, notably by Jahr (1979) in a paper in Norwegian entitled 'Er det sånn jeg snakker?' (Do I speak like that?) (see also Jahr, 1978). Jahr analysed his use of a number of syntactic variables as an interviewer for *Talmålsundersøkelsen* (investigation of spoken language: abbreviated TAUS) *i Oslo*. He concludes that his syntax was to a certain extent influenced by the sex of his informants and also by their syntax.

Analysis of my own recordings revealed that accommodation of a rather dramatic phonological sort did indeed take place. Figure 1.4 shows the scores for the variable (t) that were obtained by ten of the informants in the Norwich study. (These informants have been selected from the total sample of 60 for the purpose of this study to give (t) scores across the whole range.) Figure 1.4 also shows the (t) scores obtained by myself in interviews with each of these informants.

The variable (t) refers to the pronunciation of intervocalic and word-final /t/ as in *better* and *bet* and has three variants:

$$(t)-1 = [t]$$
$$(t)-2 = [t\underline{?}]$$
$$(t)-3 = [\underline{?}]$$

Index scores are calculated in such a way that they range from 0, indicating consistent use of the prestige pronunciation [t], to 200 for consistent use of the low-prestige glottal-stop variant.

Figure 1.4 demonstrates a remarkable degree of coincidence between my scores and those of my informants. Clearly, accommodation has taken place. It is apparent, however, that the close approximation of the two lines as they slope across the graph has been produced by my accommodating to my informants rather than vice versa. For two of the informants, Mrs W. and Mrs B., my scores are the lower, i.e. I did not use so many glottal stops as they did. These are the two informants who

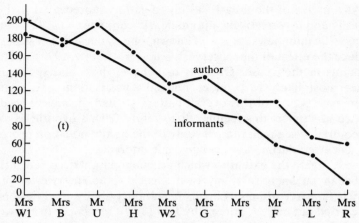

Figure 1.4   Variable (t): selected scores in author's Norwich study (Trudgill, 1974)

were lowest on the social scale and who used most glottal stops. For the other eight informants, the graph shows that I used more glottal-stop realizations of /t/ than they did, including those informants with the highest social class indices and lowest (t) scores. It is probable, I believe, that if I had been modifying my pronunciation in such a way as to induce my informants to produce pronunciations that would correlate with social class in the anticipated direction, then the cross-over pattern on the graph would have been reversed: I would have had higher (t) indices than the working-class speakers, and lower scores than the middle-class speakers.

The fact that I have higher scores than most of the informants must be ascribed to the factor of age. Glottal-stop realizations of (t) are increasing in frequency, and younger speakers typically score higher than older speakers, other things being equal. At the time of the interviews I was aged 24, and the ten informants shown here were all older than that.

Note also that the influence of the sex of the interlocutor noted by Jahr (1979) is probably at work here. From the graph it looks as if I may well have been using a higher proportion of low-prestige glottal-stop realizations of /t/ when talking to the two men than to the eight women. This is consonant with the findings of Shopen (ms.) who has found that, in Australian English at least, both men and women use more higher-status pronunciations, on average, when talking to women than when talking to men.

We can argue, then, that linguistic analysis is a useful tool in any examination of the processes involved in linguistic accommodation. This is clearly demonstrated in figure 1.5, which presents a finding that would never have been revealed by impressionistic measures of degree of accommodation. Figure 1.5 again compares my pronunciation with that of my Norwich informants, and relates to the variable (a:), which deals with the degree of fronting or backing of the vowel of the lexical set of *part*, *path*, *half*, *banana*, etc. There are three variants:

$$(a:)-1 = [ɑ:]$$
$$(a:)-2 = [ɒ:\sim ɒ̈:]$$
$$(a:)-3 = [a:]$$

Indices are calculated in such a way that consistent use of the received pronunciation (RP) back vowel [ɑ:] scores 0, and the low-prestige front variant 200.

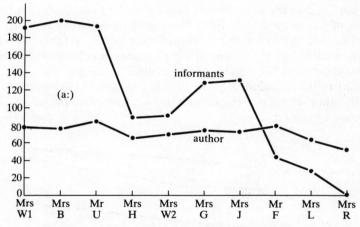

Figure 1.5   Variable (a:): selected scores in author's Norwich study (Trudgill, 1974)

Figure 1.5 shows that, although as we have just seen I did accommodate to my informants in the case of (t), I did *not* accommodate to them in my pronunciation of (a:) (or if I did, any accommodation was very slight).

Without a detailed linguistic analysis, a finding of this sort would not have been possible. If no linguistic analysis had been carried out, we would not have known for certain that, during accommodation between accents that differ at a number of points, some features are modified and some are not. Now that this fact has been attested, the very interesting question arises: why are some aspects of pronunciation altered during the accommodation process while others remain unchanged? If we are able to make some progress towards answering this question, we may also gain some insights into the mechanisms that come into play in dialect contact situations of the sort that we shall be observing in subsequent chapters.

Explanations for modification

The reason why Norwich (t) and (a:) behave differently during accommodation, at least in my speech, is actually fairly readily apparent. Labov has noted (1972) that in most speech communities some linguistic variables are subject to both social class and stylistic variation; these he labels *markers*. Other variables are subject simply to social class variation; these are labelled *indicators*. Now, it happens (see Trudgill, 1974) that (t) is a marker in Norwich English, while (a:) is merely an indicator. Norwich English speakers do not (see figure 1.6) change their pronunciation of /a:/ very greatly from one social situation to another. It is therefore not surprising that I myself maintained a fairly consistent (lower-middle-class type) central vowel quality for this vowel throughout the interviews. The quality of the vowel /a:/ is not sensitive to the formality of the situation. Equally, it is not sensitive to the quality of /a:/ used by other speakers. Speakers do not accommodate on /a:/ any more than they style-shift.

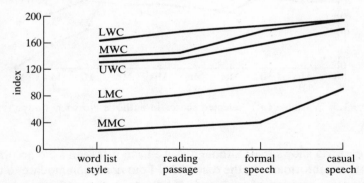

Figure 1.6   Variable (a:): by class and style (from Trudgill, 1974)

But why not? Simply to point out that (a:) is an indicator and (t) a marker is not to explain *why* this is so, or how this distinction arises in the first place. Labov suggests in fact that markers are relatively high in a speaker's consciousness, as compared to indicators. (Variables which have an especially high level of awareness associated with them are called *stereotypes*.) The high level of awareness associated with a marker leads speakers to modify their pronunciation of it in situations (such as formal occasions) where they are monitoring their speech most closely (though see Bell, 1984). The same explanation obviously works for the accommodation process: in contact with speakers of other language varieties, speakers modify those features of their own varieties of which they are most aware.

This leads, of course, to a further question: why exactly are speakers more aware of some variables than others? Our earlier Norwich research (see Chambers and Trudgill, 1980) suggested that in the absence of certain factors, at least one of which must be present, a linguistic variable will normally be an indicator. In the case of Norwich, at least, the factors which lead to greater awareness and thus to an indicator becoming a marker are the following:

(1) Greater awareness attaches to forms which are overtly stigmatized in a particular community. Very often, this overt stigmatization is because there is a high-status variant of the stigmatized
form *and* this high-status variant tallies with the orthography
while the stigmatized variant does not. Examples of this in Norwich English include Ø vs. /h/ in *hammer* etc., and /n/ vs. /ŋ/ in
walking etc.

(2) Greater awareness also attaches to forms that are currently
involved in linguistic change.

(3) Speakers are also more aware of variables whose variants are
phonetically radically different.

(4) Increased awareness is also attached to variables that are involved
in the maintenance of phonological contrasts. Thus, in Norwich,
items from the lexical set of *huge, cue, music, view, tune* may be
pronounced with either /ʉ:/ or /jʉ:/. The latter pronunciation
implies a contrast in minimal pairs such as *Hugh:who, dew:do,
feud:food* etc. The former, on the other hand, involves a loss of
this contrast.

Long-term accommodation

We are thus able to argue that, during accommodation to speakers who are members of the same immediate speech community, speakers modify their pronunciation of linguistic variables that are markers within the community. This is because of the *salience* which attaches to markers and indeed turns variables into markers in the first place. This salience is, in turn, due to factors such as those we have just outlined – to do with stigmatization, linguistic change, phonetic distance, and phonological contrast (see Timberlake, 1977; Kerswill, 1985).

The next question we would like to ask concerns the extent to which speakers accommodating to other speakers from *other* speech communities will behave in the same way (see Knops, 1981). Is it the case that, when accommodating to varieties that are *regionally* different from their own, speakers will also modify features that for them are in some way salient? It is not immediately clear that they will, since accommodation beyond the speech community will often be a rather different process from accommodation within it. Accommodation within the speech community, as in my Norwich interviews, involves altering the frequency of usage of particular variants of variables over which the speaker already has control. Accommodation beyond the speech community, on the other hand, may well involve the adoption of totally new features of pronunciation.

We move now to an investigation of this issue, with particular reference to the question of whether it is *salient* linguistic features that are modified in all types of accent convergence. We do this by examining a not uncommon type of long-term, extra-speech community accommodation in the English-speaking world, namely accommodation by speakers of English English to American English as a result of residence in the United States.

In carrying out this investigation, we are naturally concerned to establish exactly what are the features of American English that are most prominent in the consciousness of English English speakers, for whatever reason. This, in fact, is a relatively simple task as far as phonology is concerned. Obviously the most salient features of American English pronunciation, for English people, are precisely those which are reproduced during *imitation*. Most speakers of English English do not of course spend much of their lives imitating American English, but there are a number of speech events where this does happen, such as the telling of jokes involving Americans, and the playing of American roles by English actors. Perhaps, however, the most obvious site for the study of the imitation of American English by English English speakers lies in the linguistic behaviour of British pop singers.

It can readily be noted that singers of this type of music observe to a remarkable extent a number of rules concerning the way in which the words of pop and rock songs should be pronounced. The strength with which these rules apply varies considerably from singer to singer and time to time, but it is clear that most such singers employ different accents when singing than when speaking. It is also clear that, whatever the speaking accent, the singing accent is one which is influenced by American English pronunciation. The process that is involved in this phenomenon, moreover, is obviously *imitation* and not *accommodation*.

In modifying their accents as they do, singers render their pronunciation *less* like that of their British audiences, not more.

Analysis of the pronunciation used by British pop singers, from the late 1950s to the late 1970s, shows that the following aspects of American English pronunciation are widespread, normal or even compulsory (see Trudgill, 1983):

(1) Words such as *life*, *my* tend to be sung with a monophthongal vowel of the type [a·], although in spoken English English they are most usually pronounced with a diphthong of the type [aɪ~ɑɪ~ʌɪ] etc.

(2) Words such as *girl*, *more* tend to be pronounced with an /r/ even by those English English speakers (the majority) who do not have non-prevocalic /r/ in their speech.

(3) Words such as *body*, *top* may be pronounced with unrounded [ɑ] instead of the more usual British [ɒ].

(4) It is not usual to pronounce words such as *dance*, *last* with the /a:/ that is normal in the speech of south-eastern England. Instead they are pronounced with the /æ/ of *cat* (as in the north of England, although the pronunciation is usually [æ] rather than northern [a]). In addition, words such as *half* and *can't*, which are pronounced with /a:/ by most northern English speakers, must also be pronounced with /æ/. Thus:

	cat	dance	half
south-eastern England	/æ/ = [æ]	/a:/	/a:/
northern England	/æ/ = [a]	/æ/	/a:/
pop-song style	/æ/ = [æ]	/æ/	/æ/

(5) The pronunciation of intervocalic /t/ in words like *better* as [t] or [ʔ], which are the pronunciations most often used by most British speakers, is generally not used. In pop singing, a pronunciation of the type [ɾ~d] – a voiced alveolar flap – has to be employed.

Other features of American English pronunciation do occur, but they are less frequent and less widespread. Clearly, the above five features are the most common in British pop-singing style because it is these pronunciations which are most saliently characteristic of American accents for the singers and, presumably, other British (or at least English) people. (As to why British singers should *want* to imitate Americans, see Trudgill, 1983, chapter 8.)

Why these features should be salient in this way is less easy to establish, but an examination of the reasons suggested above for the growth of *markers* in Norwich English does give us some clues. The factor that has to do with ongoing linguistic change is not likely to be of relevance. But the other factors – those that have to do with phonetic distance, stigmatization, and phonological contrast – do provide some pointers. In particular, we can note a similarity between the last two: the variables affected by stigmatization often involve, as the comment above about orthography suggests, *phonological* rather than phonetic variation and alternation or contrast between surface phonemes. The (ng) variable, for instance, involves alternation between one phoneme /ŋ/ and another /n/; while (h) involves alternation between a phoneme /h/ and its absence, just as the *Hugh:who* (yu) variable involves alternation between zero and /j/. Note then that the salience of non-prevocalic /r/ in American English for English listeners may have to do with the fact that this difference between the two varieties also concerns presence of a phoneme versus its absence, while the salience of /æ/ in *dance* also involves alternation between two phonemes /æ/ and /ɑ:/ rather than a purely phonetic difference. The other three features are less easy to account for, but notice that American /ɑ/ in *hot* does sound like English /ɑ:/ in *heart* (see below), and that /t/ = [ḓ] involves *loss of phonemic contrast* between /t/ and /d/. The *phonetic distance* between [a·] and, say, [ɒɪ] is rather striking and may also be of relevance here (see point 3 below).

We may also note, as further evidence for the importance of *phonemic* alternation in leading to salience in cross-dialectal imitation, that there are a number of other American features that *could* have been salient but do not seem to be. Analysing linguists, for instance, might contrast the longer, closer realizations of /æ/ common in many varieties of American English, as in *bad* [bɛ·ᵊd], with the more open, shorter variants found in England, as in [bæd]. Imitation by pop singers, however, typically does not involve this feature which is, from an English English point of view, purely phonetic.

If we then accept imitation as a good guide to the degree of salience of American pronunciation features for English listeners, we can now move on to an examination of whether it is in fact these salient features which are also, as we might want to predict, accommodated to when English English speakers come into contact with Americans.

The data on which this examination is based is perhaps a little unusual. There are two main data sets. The first consists of notes made by myself on the segmental phonology of native speakers of English English who have been or are living in the United States. These notes are based on informal observations of speakers mostly engaged in academic occupations, and were often made, I confess, at conferences and during lectures. There are, of course, dangers to be aware of in working with data from such a restricted social base, but the notes are numerous enough – and contain sufficient observations on nonacademics – for me to believe that this is not a serious cause for concern. The second set consists of observations of what happened to my own speech when, as a native speaker of English English, I spent a year living in the USA. There are of course obvious worries about informal, untaped investigations of one's own speech. I attempted, however, to ensure that the data was as 'clean' as possible by noting pronunciations employed by me in a relatively unconscious way and that I, as it were, caught myself saying unawares. (Many linguists are, I believe, familiar with the phenomenon of realizing that they have said something of linguistic interest only *after* they have said it.) Linguistics colleagues were also kind enough, from time to time, to point out Americanisms in my speech.

My notes show that it is indeed the features singled out by pop singers – and for the most part no other features – that are modified during accommodation. A comparison of imitation by pop singers with accommodation by expatriates, as far as the five main features are concerned, shows the following:

(1) /ai/: [aɪ] > [a·] as in *life*. This feature of British pop-singing style is not in imitation of Americans as a whole, but rather of Southerners and/or Blacks. (Many American Blacks have monophthongal realizations of /ai/. This pronunciation is also very widespread in the speech of Whites in the American South. In some areas, such as parts of Virginia, it occurs before voiced consonants or word-finally only, while in other areas of the South it is found in all environments.) Indeed, many American singers who have a diphthongal pronunciation of /ai/ in their speech also adopt the monophthong when singing, in imitation of Blacks and/or Southerners. During my time in the USA I was not in the South or in close contact with Blacks or Southerners. It is therefore not surprising that I, like most other English visitors to America, did not acquire this feature. Nor did any of my other informants.

(2) /r/: Ø > /r/ /__{#, C} as in *cart*. During my stay in the USA there were no signs at all of any acquisition of non-prevocalic /r/. I did occasionally pronounce /r/ in this position, but this was done deliberately and consciously to avoid confusion between, say, *Bob* and *Barb*, my English pronunciation of the latter often being taken by Americans as the former. My notes in fact suggest that the vast majority of non-rhotic adult English English speakers in the USA do not acquire this feature until they have been in America for a considerable period (say ten years or so), if at all. Those that do acquire it certainly acquire other American English features first, and acquire it, too, in an inconsistent and/or lexically conditioned and/or not entirely accurate manner (see chapter 2). One of my informants, resident in the USA for ten years,

was consistent in pronouncing /r/ only in the words *for*, *where*, *here*, and *are*, and with a couple of very rare exceptions pronounced non-pre-vocalic /r/ nowhere else, not even in *aren't*.

It seems, then, that /r/, though apparently salient, is not readily accommodated to. Why should this be? Is our hypothesis incorrect? The answer appears to be that, while salience (as indicated by imitation) is indeed crucial, as we have argued, it is not the whole story. Salient features will be accommodated to *unless* other factors intervene to delay, inhibit or even prevent accommodation. In this particular case the inhibiting factor would appear to be a *phonotactic constraint*. Non-rhotic English English accents, obviously, have a phonotactic rule which permits /r/ to occur only before a vowel, and prevents its occurrence pre-consonantally and pre-pausally.

Now there is plenty of evidence available to indicate that phonotactic constraints of this type are very strong, and cause considerable difficulty in foreign language learning. Broselow (1984), for instance, argues that in second-language acquisition 'syllable structure restrictions are particularly susceptible to transfer', and suggests the following *syllable structure transfer hypothesis*:

> When the target language permits syllable structures which are not permitted in the native language, learners will make errors which involve altering these structures to those which would be permitted in the native language.

Thus, English speakers who have no trouble at all pronouncing [ŋ] in *sing* etc. have considerable difficulty with word-initial [ŋ] in, say, Burmese, and convert forms such as *Nkomo* [ŋkomo] found in African languages to forms such as [ənkoumou] that conform to English patterns.

There seems to be no reason at all why these difficulties should not also apply to second-*dialect* acquisition and to the accommodation process. I can certainly attest that if I want to pronounce, say, *part* as /pärt/ I find it very hard to do so in the flow of conversation, and it is worthy of note that even those British pop singers who appear to be trying hardest to imitate American singers nevertheless rarely achieve an /r/ – pronunciation rate of higher than 50 per cent (see Trudgill, 1983) even though, one assumes, they are usually performing songs that they have rehearsed and sung many times before. We can claim, therefore, that although non-prevocalic /r/ is indeed a salient feature of American English for English people, the phonotactic constraint present in their non-rhotic accents prevents them from accommodating to American English on this particular feature.

(3) /ɒ/: /ɒ/ > /ɑ/. Again there was no trace of any tendency in my speech to modify the pronunciation of *hot*, *top* etc. from [hɒt] to [hɑt]. This is more difficult to explain, since the change could be interpreted as being a purely phonetic one involving no phonotactic constraints. It is possible, however, that the answer to the question of why this modification was not made lies instead in the notion, well known to students of dialectology, of *homonymic clash*. English English already has a vowel of the low back unrounded [ɑ] type in the lexical set of *heart*, *park*, *calm*, *half* etc. It is true that this vowel in my speech, approximately [ɑ̟:], is not absolutely identical with the vowel many Americans have in *hot*, *top* etc., approximately [ɑ̟~ɑ̟]. But it is close enough to cause confusion, as in the case of my *Barb* being interpreted as American English *Bob*, mentioned above. Certainly, if I try to say *hot* in the American manner, it feels to me as if I were saying *heart*. The wholesale adoption of the American vowel would thus have led to the loss of contrast between pairs such as:

hot	*heart*
pot	*part*
cod	*card* etc.

Just as the possibility of the loss of contrast can prevent the occurrence of sound changes, so apparently can it influence accommodation. In other words, it is precisely the same characteristics of /ɑ/ as make it salient, and therefore a candidate for accommodation, that delay (although not prevent – mergers do occur!) its accommodation. A similar phenomenon occurs in the English of Belfast (J. Milroy, personal communication), where speakers accommodating upwards do not generally change /eɪ/ [e:] to [eɪ] in *lane* etc. because [eɪ] already occurs as a realization of /aɪ/ in *line* etc.

There are, however, other factors one should perhaps consider. For instance, the relationship between English English /ɒ/ and US English /ɑ/ is not entirely straightforward. In many varieties of US English, some words which in English English have /ɒ/ actually have /ɔ/ rather than /ɑ/: *lost*, *long*, *off* etc. Other words which have /ɒ/ in English English have /ʌ/ in US English: *of*, *what*, *was*, etc. Successful accommodation would therefore be a somewhat complex process.

Secondly, Labov has suggested (personal communication) that a further inhibiting factor in my own case may be that [ɑ] is also a conservative, rural, low-status pronunciation in Norfolk, the English county of which I am a native.

The rest of my data indicates, in any case, that while English English speakers do in fact accommodate on this feature more readily than they do on /r/, it still takes some considerable time before accommodation begins.

(4) /a:/ < /æ/ in *dance, last* etc. The data indicates that this is a change which English English speakers do make reasonably early on, if they are going to accommodate in the long term to US English. Even speakers from the north of England, moreover, can be perceived to accommodate on this feature. First, the vowel in words such as *half* and *can't* changes from /a:/ to /æ/ and, secondly, the phonetic realization of /æ/ changes from [a] to [æ~æ·], e.g. [last] > [læ·st] *last* (southern English English [lɑ:st]). In my own speech there was some trace of accommodation on this feature (see below), though much of it was at a relatively conscious level and occurred only in certain situations.

This feature would seem to be a very obvious candidate for change during accommodation, since it involves a very simple modification. English English speakers already have the vowel /æ/ in their inventory, and it would therefore be a very simple matter to substitute this for /a:/ and say /dæns/ rather than /da:ns/. Southern English English has *romance* /roumæns/, so why not /dæns/? It has *ant* /ænt/, so why not *plant* /plænt/?

It is therefore not easy to explain the delay that occurs in the acquisition of this feature amongst those English English speakers who accommodate to US English. Introspection, however, suggests a sociopsychological explanation, at least in my own case. Since this explanation stems from introspection, it may not be applicable in other cases, although informal discussions have indicated that other people may have the same experience. The explanation lies in the fact that the vowel /æ/ in this lexical set is *too* salient an American feature. It is not adopted immediately because it sounds, and feels, *too American*. The stereotype is too strong. (Why this is, it is hard to say, but note again that alternation between phonemes is involved: see below.)

Other similar phenomena can be noted, even if they have not yet been studied in any systematic way. In England, 'Northerners' are stereotyped by 'Southerners' as saying *butter* etc. as /butə/ rather than /bʌtə/, and as saying *dance* /dæns/ rather than /da:ns/. 'Southerners', on the other hand, are stereotyped by 'Northerners' as saying /da:ns/ rather than /dæns/, while the pronunciation of *butter* appears to be of relatively little significance and is rarely commented on. It is therefore interesting to note that Northerners moving to the South and accommodating to Southern speech usually modify *butter* /butə/ to /bʌtə/ or at least to /bətə/, but much less rarely modify /dæns/ to /da:ns/. Many Northerners, it seems, would rather drop dead than say /da:ns/: the stereotype that this is a Southern form is again *too strong*.

The argument given above for suggesting that the modification of /a:/ to /æ/ (and therefore also *vice versa*) should be an easy one to make because of the prior existence of the required phoneme in the system, may in fact be precisely the explanation for why these changes are *not* made. If differences between two accents involve simply the *incidence* of a particular phoneme in a given lexical set, then that difference will be very highly salient – and maybe too salient – since speakers are conditioned to tune in to features that are phonemic in their own variety. English English speakers are highly aware of US English /æ/ in *dance* because they themselves have /æ/ in *romance*. Southern English English speakers are highly aware that Northern English English speakers say *butter* /bʊtə/ because they themselves have /ʊ/ in /pʊt/. Northern speakers are highly aware that Southern speakers say /da:ns/ because they themselves have /a:/ in *calm, half, car, banana* etc. On the other hand, they are *not* so aware of the Southern *butter* /bʌtə/ pronunciation since they have no such vowel as /ʌ/.

(5) /t/: [t] > [d̪]. My notes indicate that this is a feature which is accommodated to very early on by many speakers of English English in North America. It is also a modification that took place relatively rapidly in my own speech – not consistently, but to a considerable extent. This is not difficult to account for, especially since the inhibiting factors we have discussed in (2)–(4) above appear not to be present. First, the change is a purely phonetic one involving no phonological complications. Intervocalic /t/ simply becomes realized as [d̪]. Secondly, no homonymic clash is involved. For example, in my own speech *latter* and *ladder* remained distinct as [læd̪ə] and [lædə]. (This, of course, is not what happens in many genuine American accents, where the contrast between /t/ and /d/ is neutralized intervocalically, both being realized as [d̪]: see above.) Thirdly, the flap [d̪] is actually already available in my native accent. (It is also common in London varieties of English, as a more formal alternative to [ʔ] for intervocalic /t/, and is widespread in south-western and Welsh (see above) varieties, especially rural dialects, as the most usual realization of this consonant.) In many East Anglian varieties, there is a phonotactic constraint (which does not occur in, for example, London English) whereby a glottal stop may not occur both before and after an unstressed /ɪ/ or /ə/. Thus, while *get* is [gɛʔ] and *it* is [ɪʔ], and *get him* is [gɛʔɪm~gɛʔəm], *get it* cannot be *[gɛʔɪʔ]. In cases such as these the pronunciation has to be [gɛd̪ɪʔ] (or the more formal [gɛtɪʔ~gɛtɪt]). The fact that the phone is reasonably widespread already in some varieties of English English has the consequence that it is not too strongly stereotyped as being American. The fact that it is already available in my own speech in intervocalic position meant that there was

no difficulty in my extending it to all intervocalic positions. Finally, it is also worth noting that the pronunciation of intervocalic /t/ in many British English accents – indeed increasingly in all accents except those of the north-west, the west midlands, the south-west and most of Wales, and high-status accents everywhere – has become problematical. Speakers can either select the variant [t], which is socially marked as being careful, formal, posh, upper class etc., or [ʔ], which is socially marked as being careless, informal, rough, lower class etc. The use of the flap [ḍ] is a convenient way out of having to select a pronunciation which is socially marked in one way or another. (For most speakers, [ʔ] as a realization of *word-final* /t/ is not nearly so salient and occurs much more frequently and higher up the social scale than the more conspicuous intervocalic /t/.)

The overall picture, then, is that the majority of English English speakers accommodating to American English follow exactly the same route. There is no way, of course, of predicting how fast and how far individuals will accommodate, if indeed they accommodate at all. This, we can assume, will depend on a number of factors, including personality type. What we can say is that *if* they accommodate, they will almost certainly accommodate phonologically by acquiring features in a certain order. The order is:

(1) -/t/- > -[ḍ]-
(2) /a:/ > /æ/ in *dance* etc.
(3) [ɒ] > [ɑ] in *top* etc.
(4) Ø > /r//__{C# }

Thus, English people resident in the USA who pronounce *top* as [tʰɑp] will also certainly have at least some tendency to pronounce *dance* etc. with /æ/, while the reverse is not necessarily the case. All my informants, in fact, conform to this pattern, with accommodation to a given feature implying accommodation also to those features lower on the hierarchy, but not necessarily to higher features. (One apparent exception to this pattern was an Englishwoman who had lived in the USA for over ten years and who had non-prevocalic /r/ and /ɒ/ as [ɑ] but who did *not* have /æ/ in the lexical set of *dance*. It emerged, however, that most of her time in America had been spent in eastern New England where, as in England, *dance* has the vowel of *pa* and not of *pat*.)

Our hypothesis is therefore confirmed, if in modified form. Accommodation does indeed take place by the modification of those aspects of segmental phonology that are *salient* in the accent to be accommodated to. This salience is revealed by what happens during imitation, and can most likely be mainly accounted for by the involvement of phonemic contrasts and alternations. There are, however, a number of factors which intrude to delay or prevent, to different extents, the acquisition of particular salient features. The factors include phonotactic constraints in particular, but also the possibility of homonymic clash and strength of stereotyping. These factors produce, in two-accent contact, a hierarchy of features such that those with the fewest or weakest inhibiting factors are accommodated to first, regardless of the actual speed of accommodation of a given individual.

Comprehensibility

In any examination of the routes followed by individual speakers during accommodation, there is another important factor that we have to discuss. This is a factor which has been of little interest to social psychologists but must be of relevance to linguists: the need to be understood. We are concerned here, of course, with interaction between related varieties where mutual intelligibility is not usually a serious or long-term problem. It can, however, be a short-term problem in some cases, and speakers in this sort of situation rapidly acquire an awareness that some features are likely to cause interlocutors more trouble than others (see Haugen's 1966 discussion of intra-Scandinavian communication).

This point, and its influence on accommodation, has been investigated by Shockey (ms.) in her examination of long-term accommodation by middle-class Americans living in England to English English, the reverse of the process we have been discussing above. She observes that the speech of long-term American residents in England is characterized by three main modifications:

(1) The pronunciation of /ou/ as in *boat* becomes fronted from [o·ʊ] to [ɵʉ], a feature of modern RP. Whether this aspect of the RP accent is salient for American speakers to the same extent as certain other more phonemic features is not clear, as it represents a modification that is purely phonetic. As such, however, it is subject to no inhibiting factors. (There are, of course, a number of areas of the USA where front or central realizations such as [øʉ~ɵʉ] occur, particularly in Philadelphia, along the central east coast, and in the inland south, but Shockey's informants all came from the midwest or California and did not have this feature natively.)

(2) The pronunciation of the vowel of *hot*, *top* etc. as rounded [ɒ], as in most British accents, rather than as the unrounded [ɑ] typical of most American accents. This, of course, is the reverse of the

process that occurs during accommodation in the opposite direction, suggesting that the contrast between [ɒ] and [ɑ], which is indeed phonetically one of the sharpest differences between the two varieties, is salient for both sets of speakers. Degree of phonetic distance between phones must surely be a factor contributing to salience (see above; and Thelander, 1979, p. 108). However, unlike the change in the reverse direction, the change by American speakers from [ɑ] to [ɒ] produces no likelihood of homonymic clash.

(3) The intervocalic flap [ɖ] is modified to [t] in the set of *latter* and to [d] in the set of *ladder*. Shockey has some interesting data on this feature from recordings of her own speech:

percentage [ɖ]	/t/	/d/
after six months in England	100	100
after three years in England	66	77

She points out that even after three years her scores are higher than those of her informants (see below), and suggests that accommodation must be a slow, ongoing process which is not completed for a number of years. Note also that Shockey was much slower in losing flaps than I and my English informants were in acquiring them. This points to another factor which must be of importance in influencing the rate of accommodation on particular features: the relative naturalness of a phonetic/phonological change. The voicing of intervocalic voiceless stops, as in moving from British to American English, is a very well-attested, natural and phonetically motivated type of sound change. The reverse process, as in moving from American to English English, whereby voiced stops become voiceless in intervocalic contexts, is neither natural nor well known as a linguistic change. It is therefore not surprising if English-to-American accommodation takes place much earlier with respect to this feature than American-to-English accommodation.

Now Shockey's analysis of tape-recorded interviews with her informants shows that all of them are variable with respect to this feature, and interestingly that, as in her own speech, /t/ and /d/ are affected differently:

percentage flaps	/t/	/d/
informant 1	17	61
informant 2	37	58
informant 3	41	67
informant 4	39	68

Flaps have been reduced, as a result of accommodation to English

English, from a presumed original score of 100 per cent in both cases, but the reduction is much greater in the case of /t/ than in the case of /d/.

Shockey rightly makes the point, in attempting to explain this fact, that students of accommodation must recognize that, in addition to the sociopsychological factors which lie at the root of accommodation (such as the desire not to be too different), the desire to be intelligible is also an important factor. American and British English, particularly the more standard varieties, are very readily mutually intelligible, but difficulties do arise from time to time. Shockey points out that comprehension of TV programmes from across the Atlantic often relies on context. It is, moreover, in situations where no context is provided (and where the listener has not had time to work out which variety the speaker is using) that misunderstanding occurs. These situations are often service encounters. Shockey reports that vowel differences have led to her receiving *cherries* (EngEng [čɛɹɪz]) in England when she asked for *carrots* AmEng [kɛɹəts], EngEng [kæɹəts]). She also reports, however, that it is the flapping of intervocalic /t/ which seems to cause British listeners the greatest comprehension difficulties. Flapping of /d/, on the other hand, is much less of a problem because of the close phonetic similarity of American [ḍ] and English [d]. The desire to make oneself more easily understood is therefore at least partly responsible for the differential modification during accommodation of /d/ and /t/.

There is also evidence for the obvious effect of comprehension as a factor in accommodation to American English by speakers of English English. I can attest that one factor that without doubt precipitated the introduction of flaps into my own speech in America was the number of people who thought, for example, if only for a second, that I wanted a *pizza* rather than that my name was *Peter*. And, while I did not generally change /a:/ to /æ/ in the lexical set of *dance* etc., I did end up saying words such as *glass*, *half*, and *bathroom* with /æ/ in service encounters in shops, bars, and restaurants, in order to avoid exchanges of the type below:

Waiter: Would you care for another bottle of wine?
Author: A half bottle, please.
Waiter: Coffee?

The problem was of course that the /a:/ in *half* sounded to the waiter more like his own vowel in *coffee* than the expected /æ/ vowel of *half*.

The accommodation process

We have argued that, at least in contact between American and English English, accommodation follows a fixed route. If it is the case that regularities of this sort are to be found in other accommodation situations, then this opens up the possibility not only that we will be able to make sensible generalizations about the accommodation process as a whole, but also that it might be possible, given a comparison of two varieties, to *predict* what form accommodation between them will take. If this is so, then it might even be possible to predict and explain which features will survive, or not, in dialect contact and dialect mixture situations also (see chapter 3).

Further evidence on the regularity of the accommodation process comes from the work of Nordenstam (1979). Nordenstam has examined long-term linguistic accommodation by Swedish women living in Bergen, Norway, to Norwegian. This is a situation somewhat comparable to that of British speakers residing in the USA. Swedish and Norwegian have a very high degree of mutual intelligibility, and Swedes do not for the most part need to modify their speech greatly when communicating with Norwegians in order to be understood. However, it is clear that the degree of intelligibility (see Haugen, 1966) depends on a number of factors – the variety of Swedish/Norwegian spoken, the degree of education, the degree of willingness to communicate, and so on – and is probably somewhat smaller than that between at least standard American and English English. It is also apparent that the fact that Norwegian and Swedish are two autonomous, separate languages – and are perceived as such by their speakers – is of some consequence. Some of the Swedes studied by Nordenstam, for example, were clearly attempting to keep the two languages apart and become bilingual, rather than introduce Norwegian features piecemeal into their Swedish. This does not normally happen within the English-speaking world, except at times in the case of bidialectal children, since there is no perception that, say, American and English standard English are discretely autonomous varieties and that they therefore *ought* to be kept apart. Rather, the autonomy is *shared* (see Chambers and Trudgill, 1980).

Nordenstam's study is mainly lexical and morphological, and indeed it is at these two levels that the two languages differ most. (Syntactic differences are very few, and pronunciation differences between the two, though clear enough to most Scandinavians, are probably no greater than differences *within* the two languages.) This contrasts with differences between English and American English, where there are hardly any morphological differences (and what there are are mostly tendencies rather than absolute differences); a number of important syntactic and phonological differences; and a very considerable number of lexical differences (see Trudgill and Hannah, 1982).

Nordenstam finds that it is at the lexical level that accommodation begins first. This is also obviously the case with English/American accommodation. It is also clear why this is the case. Lexical differences are highly salient, and are readily apparent to all speakers of the varieties concerned without any linguistic training or analysis. They are also (mostly) non-systematic, and susceptible to being learned one at a time. Crucially, they can also cause severe, and obvious, comprehension difficulties. Indeed, in both Scandinavia and the English-speaking world there is a fund of folk knowledge about lexical differences which is shared by most adults. It is widely known in Britain, for instance, that certain lexical items and phrases are to be avoided when talking to Americans, e.g. *rubber* (EngEng 'eraser', USEng 'condom'); *to knock up* (EngEng 'to awaken by knocking', USEng 'to make pregnant'). It is similarly widely known in Scandinavia that e.g. *rolig* means 'peaceful' in Norwegian but 'amusing' in Swedish. There are also, of course, many other differences that are not known, but these are generally soon learnt when the new variety is encountered (unless ambiguity is possible, e.g. *pavement* (USEng 'roadway', EngEng 'sidewalk')).

In Nordenstam's study, lexical accommodation is followed by morphological accommodation. This is not the case with English/American accommodation, of course, where phonological accommodation comes next. English English speakers in the USA, for instance, may end up using forms such as *gotten* and *dove* (for *dived*), but this is usually preceded by at least some phonological modifications. We can probably ascribe the situation described by Nordenstam to the far greater salience, due in turn to greater frequency, of morphological differences between Norwegian and Swedish, and/or to the relative lack of phonological uniformity within and differentiation between Swedish and Norwegian.

At a number of points, Nordenstam's data shows that her Swedish subjects do indeed follow a regular and common route towards Norwegian during morphological accommodation. The majority of her informants, as the implicational scale of table 1.1 shows, acquire Norwegian-style pronouns in the following order. First, Swedish *jag* /jɑ/ 'I' is replaced by Norwegian *jeg* /jei/. Secondly, Swedish *dom* 'they' is replaced by Norwegian *de* /di:/. Thirdly, Swedish *honom* 'him' is replaced by *ham*. And finally, Swedish *ni* 'you (plural)' gives way to *dere* /de:rə/. (Many of the other pronominal forms are identical or very similar, such as *vi* 'we', *hon* (Swedish)/*hun* (Norwegian) 'she'.) In the 88-cell table, only four are 'incorrectly' ordered, although it must be conceded that eight of the informants show no accommodation at all, so perhaps we should say four out of 56. It is difficult, in view of the similarity or identity of the other forms in the system, to attempt to *explain* this ordering. But the salience of the first-person singular is not entirely unexpected, particularly since the phonetic form of the Swedish *jag* could be interpreted by Norwegians in some contexts as *ja* 'yes', while the delay in acquiring *dere* could well be due to the fact that *ni* is the polite pronoun of address in Swedish.

Table 1.1   Norwegian and Swedish pronouns

	jeg/jag	*de/dom*	*ham/honom*	*dere/ni*
Fanny	N	N	N	N
Jenny	N	N	N	N
Katarina	N	N	N	N
Bodil	N	N	N	S
Eva	N	N	N	S
Blenda	N	N	S	<u>N</u>
Charlotte	N	N	S	<u>N</u>
Henny	N	N	S	S
Carin	N	S	<u>N</u>	S
Stina	N	S	<u>N</u>	S
Barbro	N	S	S	S
Lisbeth	N	S	S	S
Alma	N	S	S	S
Nancy	N	S	S	S
Erna	S	S	S	S
Ellen	S	S	S	S
Inez	S	S	S	S
Helen	S	S	S	S
Mona	S	S	S	S
Nina	S	S	S	S
Linda	S	S	S	S
Lena	S	S	S	S

Source: Nordenstam, 1979.

At a number of other points, on the other hand, it is difficult to find any regularity at all. This can be illustrated by table 1.2. Both Norwegian and Swedish express adjectival agreement by suffixing *-t* to neuter adjectives. Plural adjectives take Swedish *-a*, Norwegian *-e*. The suffix *-a/-e* also occurs in the definite singular, e.g. *den store mannen* 'the big man'. The neuter forms of adjectives also function as adverbs. There is, however, a difference concerning adjectives with the common ending *-ig*, e.g. Norwegian *farlig* 'dangerous', *fattig* 'poor', etc. In Swedish these are treated like any other adjective. In Norwegian, on the other hand, they do not take neuter *-t*; thus accommodation involves *det är* *farligt* > *det er farlig*. In Bergen Norwegian, moreover, plural adjectives take -*e* only in attributive position. Thus accommodation from Swedish requires *dom är fina* > *de er fin*.

Table 1.2   Norwegian and Swedish adjectival agreement

	Adverb -*ig*/-*igt*	Neuter adj. -*ig*/-*igt*	Pred. adj. pl. Ø/-*e*~*a*
Fanny	N	N	S
Jenny	N	N	N
Katarina	S	N	N
Bodil	N	N	N
Eva	N	S	N
Blenda	N	N	N
Charlotte	N	N	N
Henny	S	N	S
Carin	N	S	N
Stina	N	N	N
Barbro	N	S	N
Lisbeth	N	N	N
Alma	N	S	N
Nancy	S	S	N
Erna	N	N	S
Ellen	N	S	S
Inez	S	S	S
Helen	N	N	S
Mona	N	N	S
Nina	S	S	N
Linda	N	N	S
Lena	S	S	S

Source: Nordenstam, 1979.

Table 1.2 shows that those speakers who have accommodated most to Norwegian in table 1.1 are also for the most part those who have accommodated most here, and vice versa. However, there is no way in which table 1.2 can be reordered into anything approaching an implicational scale. There is no regularity here. It is perfectly possible, of course, that we are grouping together three features which should not be grouped together, but there are in Nordenstam's work a number of other points at which the same type of phenomenon occurs. In fact, much of her data suggests quite strongly that, while there are constraints and regularities in linguistic accommodation, there is also, as in child language acquisition and in second-language learning, plenty of room for individual strategies. This is quite comforting, in a way, but disturbing for our hypothesis that accommodation takes place by means of a fixed route.

Irregularity in accommodation

It could be claimed, of course, that morphology and phonology are likely to behave differently in accommodation. Unfortunately for our fixed-route hypothesis, however, there is some evidence that even in phonology regularity is not the whole story. For example, we have data on long-term linguistic accommodation by children which shows very clearly the extent to which individual routes can be followed. The evidence is all the more striking because it comes from the linguistic behaviour of twins. The data is as follows.

Debbie and Richard were born and grew up in Britain. At the age of seven they went with their parents from Reading, in the south of England, where they had lived for a number of years, to Australia, where they stayed for one year before returning home. In Australia, recordings were made of their speech at monthly intervals for six months by Inge Rogers of Macquarie University, and these recordings were subsequently kindly made available to me.

The recordings make it possible to carry out a longitudinal study of the accommodation process through which the twins adapted their Reading phonology to that of Australian English. (Doubtless lexical accommodation occurred also. Grammatical differences between Australian and English English are so few as to be impossible to study in this way.)

Rogers (1981) showed that the twins quite rapidly acquired the distinctively Australian high-rising statement intonation. My own researches (Trudgill, 1982) investigated their accommodation at the level of segmental phonology. The main consonantal and vocalic features modified by the twins during the six-month period were as in table 1.3.

Table 1.4 shows Richard's development over the six-month period. Note the very regular pattern, and the almost entirely perfect implicational scaling. Table 1.5 shows the long-term accommodation by Richard's twin sister Debbie. The contrast is quite striking. First, Debbie has been much less regular than Richard. Secondly, the routes the two children have followed to acquiring an Australian accent have in many respects been rather different. After six months they sound, at least to a non-Australian, very Australian, but they have got to this stage via different paths. Moreover, even though she got off to a slower

Table 1.3   Main consonantal and vocalic modifications

			English (Reading)	Australian
1	-/t/-	better	[tʰ]	[ɾ]
2	/ai/	high	[ɑɪ]	[ɑ·ⁱ]
3	/ou/	low	[ɔu]	[æ·ᵘ]
4	/ei/	face	[ɛɪ]	[æ·ⁱ]
5	/i:/	see	[ɪi]	[əɪ]
6	/ʌ/	but	[ə]	[æˡ]
7	/ɑ:/	part	[ɑ̞:]	[a:]
8	/u:/	boot	[ʉ:]	[ʉʉ]
9	[ɛ]	bed	[ɛ]	[e]
10	[ɑu]	how	[æ̞u]	[ɛ·ᵘ]
11	-/t/	get	[ʔ]	[tʰ]
12	/æ/	bat	[æ]	[ɛ]
13	/ɛə/	there	[ɛ:]	[e:]
14	/ɪ̈/	David	/ɪ/	/ə/
15	/ɪ/	hit	[ɪ]	[i]

Source: Trudgill, 1982.

Table 1.4   Richard

Month	-/t/-	/ai/	/ou/	/ei/	/i:/	/ʌ/	/ɑ:/	/u:/	/ɛ/	/ɑu/	-/t/	/æ/	/ɛə/	/ɪ̈/	/ɪ/
1	A	AB	AB	B	B	B	B	B	B	B	B	B	B	B	B
2	A	AB	AB	AB	A̲	AB	AB	B	B	B	B	B	B	B	B
3	A	A	AB	AB	AB	AB	AB	AB	AB	B	B	B	B	B	B
4	A	A	A	A	AB	AB	AB	A	AB	AB	B	B	B	B	B
5	A	A	A	A	A	A	AB	A	AB	A	A	A(B)	B	B	B
6	A	A	A	A	A	A	AB	A	AB	A	A	A(B)	B	B	B

A: Australian
B: British
AB: both forms
A(B), B(A): one instance of form in parentheses
Source: Trudgill, 1982.

start, Debbie has acquired some Australian features that Richard has not. The extent of this difference is illustrated in table 1.6, which shows the first month of acquisition by both children of each feature.

It is of course possible to attempt to account for the different *rate* of accommodation by the children by noting the sex difference and observing that, during their stay in Australia, the children's friends and activities differed quite considerably – as did their personalities.

The different *routes* they followed during accommodation, however, are more troubling. The fact that the *order* of acquisition of Australian

Table 1.5 Debbie

Month	-/t/-	/ai/	/ou/	/ei/	/i:/	/ʌ/	/ɑ:/	/u:/	/ɛ/	/ɑu/	-/t/	/æ/	/ɛə/	/ɪ/	/ɪ/
1	B	B	B	B(A̲)	B	B	B	B	B	A̲B	B	B	B	B	B
2	B(A̲)	B	B	B	B	B	B(A)	B	B	B	B(A̲)	B	B	B	B
3	B	B	A	B	B	B	AB	B	B	A	B	B	B	B	B
4	B	AB	A	B	B	B	A	B	AB	A	B	B	B	B	B
5	B	AB	A	A	B	B	A	B	A	A	B	B	A	A(B)	B
6	B(A)	A	A	A	A	A	A(B̲)	A	A	A(B̲)	B(A)	AB	A	A	AB

A: Australian
B: British
AB: both forms
A(B), B(A): one instance of form in parentheses
Source: Trudgill, 1982.

Table 1.6 Month of acquisition

Feature	Key word	Debbie	Richard
1	*better*	—	1
2	*high*	3	1
3	*low*	3	4
4	*face*	4	1
5	*see*	3	2
6	*but*	4	3
7	*part*	5	2
8	*boot*	5	—
9	*bed*	5	—
10	*how*	6	2
11	*get*	6	2
12	*bat*	6	3
13	*there*	6	5
14	*David*	6	—
15	*hit*	—	5

Source: Trudgill, 1982.

features was somewhat different for the two children is obviously a considerable difficulty for the fixed-route hypothesis, just as was Nordenstam's data. Obviously, in both these cases there seems to be clear potential for different speakers to adopt different strategies of accommodation.

The fixed-route hypothesis can, nevertheless, be defended. In the face of Nordenstam's data we are able to retreat to a position which confines the hypothesis to phonology. In the case of Debbie and

Richard, we may retreat further to a position which confines the hypo-thesis to adults, or perhaps more probably to post-adolescents. Clearly, accommodation by children may be a very different kind of phenome-non from accommodation by adults. This is particularly so given the enormously greater linguistic flexibility of young children, especially up to the age of approximately eight (see below). The *speed* of accommo-dation is greater, and of course so is the *degree*. (Note, in fact, the very large number of features accommodated to by the twins as compared with the four main features we noted for English adults in the USA.) This suggests that the constraints that delay accommodation by adults, and which thereby lead to the ordering of the acquisition of features, are not, for children, constraints at all – or at least not seriously so. Therefore, the same phenomenon of ordering does not occur. Just as young children are not inhibited by, say, phonotactic constraints in learning a foreign language, so they are equally uninhibited in acquiring a different dialect. They therefore have much more freedom and scope for accommodation, and are much less likely to conform to the same fixed pattern.

Limits to accommodation

This discussion of accommodation by young children leads us to another important and interesting question, especially since the role of young children may be vital in dialect mixture and in new-dialect formation, which we shall be looking at in later chapters. The question is: what are the limits on accommodation? Specifically, is total accommodation to a new variety possible in the long term?

Now the obvious place to look, if we are concerned with the limits on long-term accommodation, is precisely the linguistic behaviour of young children. As we have just noted, children are well known to be much more rapid and complete accommodators than adults. The explanation for this may in part be sociopsychological, but is almost certainly mostly linguistic, and is concerned with the nature of brain development and the human language faculty.

In any case, the conventional wisdom is that young children, unlike adults, are indeed capable of accommodating totally to the speech of their peers, as Debbie and Richard seemed to be at least well on their way to doing. It is a matter of common observation, and has often been noted by Labov and others, that children use the dialect and accent of their friends, and not those of their parents or teachers. Indeed this must necessarily have been the case for regionally distinct dialects to have survived in the face of geographical mobility.

There are, of course, qualifications that must obviously be made at this point. A number of children of parents who speak a variety different from that of the area in which they are living become bidialectal, and speak like their parents *as well as* like their peers; and attitudinal factors may retard or limit accommodation. Moreover, isolated individuals – extreme 'lames' in Labov's sense (1972), such as the Nathan B. discussed in some detail in Labov (1966) – may be relatively immune to peer group pressure to conform since they do not have a peer group. For example, Newbrook (1982) turned up one informant in his survey of the English spoken in the Merseyside area of England who had a considerable number of Scottish features in his speech even though he had lived all his life in the Merseyside area. The explanation for this was that the informant's mother was Scottish and, crucially, that the family belonged to a closed, isolationist religious sect. Other linguists have similar anecdotes – and I make no apology for employing anecdotes since if, on a particular topic, we have many of them and they all point in the same direction, then we cannot ignore them. I have heard recently, for example, of a child born and raised in Iowa who had a strong foreign accent; and of a child who had lived all his life in Florida but who had a noticeable New York City accent. These people, however, are obviously exceptions. In general we can accept that, at least in most western cultures, children are known, in normal circumstances, to adapt at least to an extent to the speech of their peers. (This is not necessarily a cultural universal, however: see Kazazis, 1970 for an important study of the role of family and local pride in inhibiting change in Greece.)

However, we now have some evidence to indicate that, while this piece of conventional wisdom is broadly speaking correct, the true picture is actually a little more complicated. The fact is that recent research has made available some studies which show that there are linguistic limits on the degree of phonological accommodation achievable even in the case of young children. There are three studies that we can mention here.

(1) Chambers (1980) examines changes that are taking place in the English of Toronto as far as the nature of *Canadian Raising* is concerned. Canadian Raising is the characteristic of Canadian English whereby the diphthongs /ai/ and /au/ have mid-central first elements before voiceless consonants and open first elements elsewhere, as in *out loud* [ʌut laud] and *night time* [nʌit taim] (for further discussion, see chapter 4). In his study Chambers shows, amongst other things, that there is now considerable fronting of the first element of /au/. He also studies the degree of adherence by speakers to the Canadian Raising pattern by constructing a raising index for his informants as follows:

	before voiceless consonants *e.g. out*	*elsewhere* *e.g. loud, now*
(ɑu)-0	[ɛu∼ɐu∼ʌu]	[æu∼au∼ɑu]
(ɑu)-1	[æu∼au∼ɑu]	[ɛu∼ɐu∼ʌu]

As can be seen, the index is computed in such a way that a speaker adhering strictly to the phonological rule of Canadian Raising, as most Canadians do, will score 0. On the other hand, any speaker who consistently violated the rule and had open first elements in voiceless environments, and vice versa, would, in Chambers's calculations, score 100.

Figure 1.7 shows the raising index scores in three speech styles obtained by six Toronto adults in tape-recorded interviews. Of particular

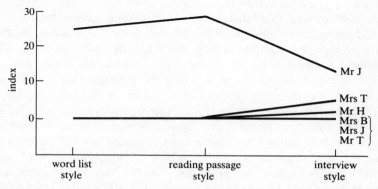

Figure 1.7   Index scores for Canadian Raising in three speech styles, Toronto (from Chambers, 1980)

interest to us are the scores obtained by Mr J. Clearly, Mr J. is doing something wrong as far as Canadian Raising is concerned. Now Chambers indicates that otherwise Mr J. speaks perfectly normal Toronto English. So why should he have trouble with Canadian Raising? The answer turns out to be that Mr J. was born in New York City and moved to Toronto only at the age of 11. Since that time he has accommodated totally to Canadian English – except at this one point, where he mostly gets things right, but not entirely. We can suggest that it is the difficulty of mastering the correct phonological constraints involved in Canadian Raising that have prevented Mr J. from acquiring the Toronto allophonic pattern completely correctly.

However, it can easily be argued that, if we are interested in the limits on accommodation by children, then the age of 11 is simply too late. I believe we can agree with this up to a point. Labov (1972) has argued

that, while children younger than eight appear to be certain to accommodate totally, there can be no assurance that, after the age of eight,
children will become totally integrated into a new speech community. I
would also add that, after the age of 14, one can be fairly sure that they
will not. The problem years are eight to 14, with the degree of inte-
gration depending on many different social and individual factors.

(2) Some pioneering work in this field by Payne (1976, 1980) has
indicated that there is a close correlation between how old speakers are
when they move to a new area and the degree to which they accommodate successfully. More interestingly, however, her work also shows
that, in some respects, even children of eight years old may be too old to
acquire certain linguistic features during long-term accommodation.

Payne's research shows that children from New York City families
who have moved to Philadelphia accommodate almost totally to the
Philadelphia sound system after residing there for a while, with the
younger children accommodating more rapidly than the older. Close
linguistic analysis, however, of the type we were advocating earlier in
this chapter, shows that there may be some inadequacies to this accommodation. The children now *sound* as if they come from Philadelphia,
but this overall impression masks the fact that they have actually failed
to master a few fine phonological details. Where the modification to be
made is purely phonetic, there are no problems for the children. For
example, the distinctively Philadelphian phonetic realizations of the
vowels /ou/ as in *boat*, /u:/ *boot*, /au/ *out*, /ai/ *bite*, and /oi/ *boy* are all
readily acquired. However, in some cases where the modifications
required are more complex phonologically, difficulties may arise. The
New York City children, for instance, show no tendency to merge the
vowels of *ferry* and *furry*, as Philadelphia speakers do (and see further
below).

(3) Clearly, then, the more complex the accommodation linguistically, the earlier the child has to begin in order to adapt successfully. Just
how early speakers have to begin to acquire certain linguistic forms
turns out, however, to be rather surprising in at least some instances. In
fact, astonishingly enough, there is some evidence to suggest that certain types of phonological differentiation may *never* be accommodated
to successfully, however young a speaker may be. The evidence is as
follows.

In the English of Norwich (see Trudgill, 1974) the originally distinct
Middle English vowels ǭ and ou have been preserved as distinct, as they
have also in a number of other (mainly geographically peripheral) areas
of Britain. The distinction in Norwich English is as follows:

ME$\bar{\varrho}$ >	/uː/	ME ou >	/ʌu/
	moan		*mown*
	nose		*knows*
	rose		*rows*
	sole		*soul* etc.

However, it is probably also relevant for what follows that the situation is further complicated by the interaction of this contrast with other vowels, especially /ʉː/ and /ʊ/, and other lexical sets. Anyone wishing to acquire native-like Norwich pronunciation has to note the existence of at least seven different lexical sets (see further chapter 3):

/jʉː/~/ʉː/	*tune* etc.
/ʉː/	*do* etc.
/ʉː/~/uː/	*boot* etc.
/uː/	*school* etc.
/uː/~/ʊ/	*road* etc.
/ʊ/	*put* etc.
/ʌu/	*own* etc.

They must learn, that is, that *do*, for example, can be pronounced only /dʉː/ = [dɜʉ], while *boot* can be pronounced either /bʉːt/ or /buːt/ = [bʊuʔ].

Now, research that I have carried out into Norwich English (see also Trudgill, 1982) indicates that even people who were born and brought up in Norwich and who otherwise have perfect local accents do not correctly master the /uː/–/ʌu/ distinction between *moan*, *mown* etc. *if their parents come from somewhere else*, i.e. if their parents do not have a Norwich accent. (In some cases, it seems to be necessary for only the mother to have had a non-Norwich accent for the distinction not to be mastered. And in one case, the distinction had not been mastered by a speaker both of whose parents did have a Norwich accent but who himself had lived away from Norwich until the age of eight, bearing out Labov's point above.)

In investigating this phenomenon, informants from Norwich aged 30–40 were used, since it is possible (see chapter 2) that younger people are now losing the /uː/–/ʌu/ distinction as a result of influence of the London area and from RP. And although the research was prompted initially by observations of natural speech, the main evidence came from tests where informants were required to repeat a sentence in 'a proper Norwich accent'. This was necessary because the RP prestige accent, as we have seen, does not make the phonological distinction in question, and 'correction' towards the RP norm is sometimes indulged in by (especially socially upwardly mobile) Norwich speakers. Absence of the distinction from their actual speech does not therefore necessarily mean that they have not mastered it correctly.

Test sentences were of the form: *Norwich City scored an own goal*. When asked to repeat this sentence in a 'proper Norwich accent', informants had no difficulty at all in comprehending what was required of them, and produced a rendering that was as basilectal as they could manage. All focused attention on producing *City* as [sɪʔɪi] and many on producing *Norwich* as [nɑɹɪj] or [nɑɹəj] rather than [nɒɹɪj]. The point of interest for this research, however, was of course the pronunciation of *own goal*. Of the ten informants with Norwich parents, all produced the correct Norwich pronunciation of *own goal* /ʌun guːl/. Of the ten with non-Norwich parents, *none* produced the correct response. In every other respect their phonetics was perfect, but they all produced /ʌun gʌul/, with the exception of one informant who had some awareness of the issue and reported that he was not sure whether *goal* should be /guːl/ or /gʌul/, but that he was 'pretty certain' that it was /gʌul/. (Interestingly, while for example (t) as in *better* is, as we saw above (p. 10), a salient variable in Norwich English and therefore subject to stylistic variation, the vowel /uː/ in *goal*, *moan* etc. has at least until very recently been subject to very little variation on the part of (particularly working-class) speakers, and has not been at all salient for local speakers. It is, on the other hand, a feature which non-locals often comment on, since the contrast between e.g. London [æˠu] and Norwich [ʊu] is very striking, and Norwich speakers moving away from the city are quickly made aware of this fact.)

It therefore appears to be the case that, probably because of the complex way in which the Norwich phonological system differs from other English systems at this point, speakers are not capable of acquiring the correct underlying phonological distinction unless they are exposed to it from the very beginning, before they themselves have even begun to speak. Exposure to it in the speech of their peers from the age of four or five is, surprising as this may seem, not sufficient.

This finding from Norwich English tallies with a finding of Payne (1976: made in fact before my own investigations, although I was regrettably not aware of this fact). However, her results are perhaps slightly less surprising than the Norwich results, since she was dealing with a new housing area with very many in-migrants, while my informants were all almost entirely surrounded in their early years by local people. She notes that the linguistic change whereby /æ/ is being raised phonetically to [ɛə~eə] causes particular problems for her New York City family children in Philadelphia. The progressive raising of /æ/ from [æː] through [ɛə] even as far as [ɪə] is taking place (see Labov, 1982), at least in urban areas, throughout the north-eastern United States, including Chicago, Detroit, Cleveland, Buffalo, Boston, New York, and Philadelphia. It is also spreading from one phonological environment to another. In Buffalo, for example, raised vowels occur in all environments, while in New York City raising is confined to vowels that occur before /m/, /n/, /s/, /θ/, /f/, /š/, /b/, /d/, /g/. In Philadelphia, the change has not progressed so far, and raised vowels occur only before /m/, /n/, /s/, /θ/, /f/, and /d/. (There is also lexical diffusion in Philadelphia in the case of the /___/d/ environment, with some words such as *bad* having close vowels, others such as *dad* having non-raised variants.) Payne shows that her informants have variable success in acquiring the correct Philadelphia pattern of /æ/ -raising, success diminishing with age of arrival in Philadelphia, and that all the originally New York City children show some tendency to have non-Philadelphia raised variants of /æ/ in *smash*, *bag*, *dad*, *grab*. The only children investigated by Payne who consistently raise /æ/ in all and only the Philadelphia environments are precisely those whose parents themselves came from Philadelphia. Again we find that a complex phonological distinction is simply not acquirable during accommodation. Speakers appear to have to learn certain phonological features from their parents. That is to say, there are clear limits on phonological accommodation, even in the case of children.

Conclusion

We have seen, then, that the quantitative linguistic analysis of the accommodation process is a useful research tool. We have seen, too, that it is at least sometimes possible to explain why some features of some accents are salient for their speakers and/or for speakers of other accents. This salience appears to be due to a number of factors, which include contribution to phonological contrast, relationship to orthography, degree of phonetic difference, and different incidence of shared phonemes. We can, moreover, perhaps reduce these factors to two, namely degree of phonetic difference and, more importantly, surface phonemic contrast. Other factors presumably remain to be detected, but in any case the salience of features can often be determined by an examination of the process of imitation. During accommodation, it is indeed salient features of the target variety that are adjusted to, except that, in the case of adults at least, a number of factors combine to delay this modification to different extents. These factors do not necessarily apply to the linguistic behaviour of children. Nor do they necessarily apply at linguistic levels other than the phonological. These factors include phonotactic constraints, homonymic clash, and extra-strong salience (both of the latter again involving, typically, surface phonemic contrasts). Other factors, on the other hand, may accelerate accommodation to particular features. These factors include comprehension difficulties and phonological naturalness. The presence of these inhibiting and accelerating factors leads, in long-term accommodation, to fixed routes whereby all speakers accommodating from one particular variety to another, whatever their speed of accommodation, acquire features from the target variety in the same order. The greater acquisitional flexibility of young children means that they are not subject to the effect of inhibiting factors to the same degree, and that they therefore demonstrate greater variety in the routes that they follow during accommodation. Even young children, however, are subject to limits on degree of accommodation, with certain more complex phonological contrasts and allophonic conditioning patterns not being acquired correctly unless speakers have been exposed to them in the speech of their parents.

2

Dialect Contact

It is a well-established fact that linguistic innovations, and linguistic forms generally, are diffused geographically from one area to another. Moreover, we understand quite a lot about how and why this type of diffusion takes place at the macro level. Geographical diffusion models have been constructed (see Chambers and Trudgill, 1980; Trudgill, 1983) that are able to make reasonably accurate predictions about the geographical routes to be followed by linguistic innovations. These models involve, crucially, a demographic factor – the population sizes of the communities involved in an interaction – and a geographical factor – the distances between the different centres.

However, we obviously know much less about how the diffusion of linguistic forms takes place at the micro level. Clearly, if a linguistic feature has spread from one region to another, it must have spread from one speaker to another, and then on to other speakers, and so on. But how *exactly* are linguistic forms transmitted from one geographical area to another *at the level of the individual speaker*?

The best explanation would appear to lie in the theory of linguistic accommodation, developed by Howard Giles, that we discussed in chapter 1. In face-to-face interaction, this explanation would have it, speakers accommodate to each other linguistically by reducing the dissimilarities between their speech patterns and adopting features from each other's speech. If a speaker accommodates frequently enough to a particular accent or dialect, I would go on to argue, then the accommodation may in time become permanent, particularly if attitudinal factors are favourable. The geographical parameter of diffusion models becomes relevant simply because, other things being equal and transport patterns permitting, people on average come into contact most often with people who live closest to them and least often with people who live furthest away. The demographic parameter becomes relevant because the larger the population of a city, the more likely an individual from elsewhere is to come into contact with a speaker from that city. For example, a speaker from Norwich (see below) is 30 to 40 times more likely to meet a Londoner than vice versa at a given time simply because the population of London is that much bigger than the population of Norwich.

It must be conceded, of course, that there is some difficulty with the suggestion made above that if accommodation, through the adoption of a feature from an alien linguistic variety, is frequent enough, then that feature may become a permanent part of a speaker's accent or dialect, even replacing original features. This is almost certainly what happens. But how often does one have to accommodate before the accommodation becomes permanent? Diffusion can be said to have taken place, presumably, on the first occasion when a speaker employs a new feature in the *absence* of speakers of the variety originally containing this feature – when, in other words, it is no longer accommodation; to use an example from chapter 1 – when a British couple resident in the USA begin using American pronunciations or expressions in their own home, when no Americans are present. Our discussion in chapter 1 leads us to suppose that individuals will actually vary enormously in the length of time they take before the new feature is permanently adopted into their speech, if at all. But we can assume the same kind of habituation process as that which must occur before accommodation takes place in the first instance. In both cases, a certain threshold will be involved: we may not, for example, change the way we pronounce a particular word until we have heard it pronounced in a different way so often that our original pronunciation begins to sound unusual and odd even to us.

In any case, we can assume that face-to-face interaction is necessary before diffusion takes place, precisely because it is only during face-to-face interaction that accommodation occurs. In other words, the electronic media are not very instrumental in the diffusion of linguistic innovations, in spite of widespread popular notions to the contrary. The point about the TV set is that people, however much they watch and listen to it, do not talk to it (and even if they do, it cannot hear them!), with the result that no accommodation takes place. If there should be any doubt about the vital role of face-to-face contact in this process, one has only to observe the geographical patterns associated with linguistic diffusion. Were nationwide radio and television the major source of this diffusion, then the whole of Britain would be influenced by a particular innovation simultaneously. This of course is not what happens: London-based innovations reach Norwich before they reach Sheffield, and Sheffield before they reach Newcastle.

There are, of course, exceptions to this. Certain highly salient linguistic features, such as new words and idioms, or fashionable pronunciations of individual words, may be *imitated* or *copied* from television or radio (rather than accommodated to). This is today, for instance, probably the primary mechanism for the adoption of American English features into British English. The phonology and grammar of modern British English varieties remain almost totally unaffected by American English, and indeed it is probable that, in terms of phonetics and phonology, British and American varieties continue to diverge quite rapidly. On the other hand, British English speakers are constantly acquiring originally American idioms and lexis. Strang (1970) lists a considerable number of items that were clearly 'Americanisms' in the 1930s but which are an integral part of British English today. These include: *bakery, grocery, bingo, cheese-cloth, raincoat, soft drinks, sweater*, and *toilet*. The older British equivalents were: *baker's shop, grocer's shop, housey-housey, butter-muslin, mackintosh, minerals, pull-over*, and *lavatory*. More recent examples include the following. From about 1970 onwards, British English speakers have increasingly used *hopefully* in the American manner, as a sentence adverbial, as in *Hopefully it won't rain today*. This usage was much attacked by self-appointed guardians of the purity of British English in the early 1970s, but is now very common indeed in the speech of a majority of British speakers. Most British speakers used the word *wireless* at least until 1960, while today nearly everybody says *radio*. The early 1980s saw the (possibly temporary) British adoption of the American expression *a whole new ball game*, even though *ball game* is never used (or even understood properly) in Britain in its literal sense. And there are also signs that the American usage of *through*, as in *Monday through Friday*, is about to begin finding its way into British usage. Very many other examples could be given. It has to be assumed that radio and especially television play a major role in the diffusion of innovations of this type, though of course written American English and face-to-face contact with Americans will also be of importance. However, precisely because face-to-face contact with Americans is a relatively rare event for most Britons, core phonology and syntax remain uninfluenced.

It is important to notice, though, that there is one situation where core syntax and phonology *can* be influenced by the media. This is where, for example, there is considerable linguistic distance between a national standard and local dialects (such as in Italy), and individual dialect speakers have made a *conscious* decision to acquire the standard. Then they may use the language of the media as a model: again, *imitation* and *copying* is the mechanism involved, and not accommodation.

Examples of diffusion

We argue, then, that the geographical diffusion of linguistic forms takes place, for the most part, when face-to-face interaction between speakers from different areas happens sufficiently frequently for accommodation to become permanent, and on a suffficiently large scale for considerable numbers of speakers to be involved. As an example we may cite the case, discussed in Trudgill (1983), of Norwich English /ɒ/=[ɑ] in *top*, *hot* etc. being replaced by [ɒ] (see p. 17). The study of this variable in apparent time, in data from my 1968 survey (see p. 44), shows clearly that the rounded vowel is becoming more prevalent amongst younger speakers, and is replacing the unrounded vowel associated with older speakers (see table 2.1). Table 2.1 also shows an interesting pattern of

Table 2.1 Norwich variable (ɒ)

Class	Sex	Word list style	Reading passage style	Formal speech	Casual speech
Middle middle	M	000	000	001	003
	F	000	000	000	000
Lower middle	M	004	014	011	055
	F	000	002	001	008
Upper working	M	011	019	044	060
	F	023	027	068	077
Middle working	M	029	026	064	078
	F	025	045	071	066
Lower working	M	014	050	080	069
	F	037	062	083	090

Source: Trudgill, 1983.

sex differentiation, with working-class males having more [ɒ] than working-class females, and yet middle-class females having more [ɒ] than males of the same class. The conclusion to be drawn from this is that the newer rounded vowel is coming into Norwich English (see map 2.1) from two different sources. First, it is entering as a prestige feature (and therefore a particularly female feature) from the RP accent. The RP-type pronunciation is coming, in the first place, into middle-class speech, precisely because it is middle-class Norwich people who have most face-to-face contact with middle- and upper-class RP speakers from Norwich and elsewhere. Secondly, it is also coming into Norwich as a non-prestige feature (and therefore a particularly male feature)

Map 2.1   East Anglian towns

from the working-class accents of surrounding areas. The working-class
pronunciation is entering Norwich, in the first instance, by means of
working-class speech, precisely because it is working-class Norwich
people who have most face-to-face contact with working-class speakers
from neighbouring towns.

Now, if it is the case that geographical diffusion results from accommodation, we would expect the factors noted in chapter 1 as being
operative during accommodation to be found also at work in the case of
geographical diffusion. In particular, we would expect *salient* features to
be diffused rather than non-salient features. And we would expect some
features to be diffused more quickly than others, depending on the
degree of salience and the number and strength of inhibiting and/or
accelerating factors, as discussed in chapter 1, that are relevant in each
case. (Geographical diffusion models can, of course, tell us to expect
forms to diffuse outwards from large cities such as Philadelphia (Labov,
1982), Liverpool (Newbrook, 1982), and London (see below). But they

cannot predict *which* features will be diffused, and which not.) Is it then the case that it actually is salient features which spread most rapidly? Is /ɒ/, for example, a salient feature for speakers in East Anglia – and is that why the pronunciation is changing?

The case of /ɒ/, in fact, is obviously a rather complex one, and we will attempt to tackle this kind of problem by examining in some detail a range of similar but simpler diffusion phenomena from our research in East Anglia. The evidence that we shall employ in this examination is as follows. During the period 1975–7, tape recordings were made of casual speech in 21 towns in the English counties of Norfolk, Suffolk, and Essex (see map 2.1), involving 348 individual speakers. In addition, 60 speakers were recorded in 1968 in the original Norwich study (Trudgill, 1974); and 15 teenagers and young adults were recorded in a follow-up study in Norwich in 1983. Analysis of these recordings, concentrating on linguistic changes taking place in this East Anglian area, have been carried out employing the apparent-time approach, which compares the speech of younger and older informants.

This analysis reveals that in recent times the diffusion of pronunciation features outwards from London into adjacent areas of East Anglia has been quite dramatic. The general diffusion of linguistic features from London is particularly noticeable in the case of the towns of Colchester, Clacton, and Walton. In these towns the older speakers sound like East Anglians, as an overall impression, while many younger speakers, as is often noted by lay observers, sound like Londoners. (In actual fact, close analysis of the speech of these younger people shows that they do, however, in many cases preserve a number of East Anglian features: see below.)

One well-known and well-studied phonological feature that has been diffused outwards from London into East Anglia within the past 150 years or so is the loss of /h/ (see J. Milroy, 1983). As has been noted before (see Trudgill, 1983), *h*-lessness is well-known not to occur in the traditional rural accents of East Anglia (see map 2.2). Our research shows, however, that *h*-dropping is now a well-established, if variable, feature of working-class urban speech in the entire East Anglian area. The feature is undergoing geographical diffusion outwards from London, and is also spreading into rural varieties, even in the north of the region. At the moment, /h/ deletion is less frequent in King's Lynn, Great Yarmouth, and Lowestoft than it is in Norwich, and less frequent in Norwich than it is in the urban centres further south. (Note that 'less frequent' here means that the feature is found in the speech of fewer individuals, and that it occurs less often in the speech of those who do have it.)

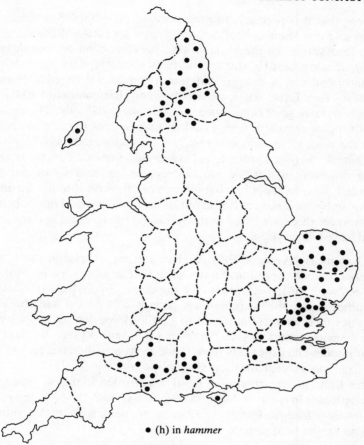

● (h) in *hammer*

Map 2.2   *h*-pronouncing areas in England (after Survey of English Dialects, Orton et al., 1962–71)

This widespread diffusion of *h*-dropping is no surprise. Our discussion of accommodation, and the relationship of accommodation to diffusion, leads us to regard *h*-dropping as a clear candidate for this type of rapid diffusion. If it is indeed features which are salient that are accommodated to – and thus subsequently diffused – then /h/ and its absence are clearly highly salient. In Norwich English itself (Trudgill, 1974) (h) as a linguistic variable is very much a *marker* (see p. 10), and of course lack of *h* is a feature which is often commented on unfavourably and overtly by teachers and others. This salience is obviously due to the phonemic contrast factor noted in chapter 1, allied to the orthography of English and social class dialect (see p. 11). In addition, it is interesting to suppose that it is precisely those aspects of (h) which lead teachers to notice and condemn lack of *h* that actually speed the diffusion of this same zero variant of the variable (cf. our discussion of American /ɑ/, p. 17). The loss of /h/ is also undoubtedly accelerated by the phonological naturalness of a change that removes a glottal fricative from the inventory (see Lass, 1984), especially when that consonant has a very restricted privilege of occurrence, i.e. syllable-initial only. The diffusion of *h*-dropping outwards from London, that is, does nothing to disabuse us of the notion that diffusion results from accommodation.

We now, therefore, turn to an examination of other features undergoing diffusion in East Anglia, as revealed in analysis of our tape-recorded data, to see if our hypotheses of diffusion through accommodation and of salience are borne out. Four features stand out as being of importance: three are listed in the following paragraphs, and the fourth merits a special section.

(1) Conservative rural East Anglian accents, at least in the north of the area, do not (or did not) have 'dark *l*' as an allophone of /l/; that is, *hill*, *bell* were [hɪl], [bɛl] rather than the more modern [hɪɫ~ɪɫ], [bɛɫ]. On the other hand, the working-class accents of London and the Home Counties (the counties adjacent to London) vocalize /l/ in the typical dark *l* environments to give *hill*, *milk* [ɪoᵈ], [mɪoᵈk] (see Wells, 1982). Even middle-class speakers from these areas usually have very marked velarization/pharyngealization and/or lip-rounding of [ɫ].

This London-area treatment of [ɫ] has also led to various interesting developments in the vowel system (see Wells, 1982), notably the merger of vowels before /l/. For many Londoners, pairs such as the following may no longer be distinct:

doll : *dole*
pull : *pool*
fill : *feel*

Even in middle-class speech, moreover, and even if complete vocalization of [ɫ] does not occur, vowels may have radically different allophones before /l/ as compared with elsewhere:

rude	[ɹʉːd]	*rule*	[ɹuːᵘɫ]
code	[kɵʉd]	*coal*	[kɔuᵘɫ]

The interaction of the older East Anglian treatment of /l/ with this newer London and Home Counties system makes for a complex pattern of change as the Home Counties system spreads. The current situation appears to be as follows (see maps 2.3 and 2.4):

(a) Distinct allophones of /u:/ and /ou/ before /l/ occur in all the towns investigated *except* Cromer, Dereham, King's Lynn, Great Yarmouth, Lowestoft, and Norwich. In Hadleigh and Stowmarket this feature is confined to younger speakers of approximately 30 and under.
(b) Strong velarization and labialization, but without complete vocalization, occur in Clacton, Walton, Colchester, Wivenhoe, Felixstowe, and Sudbury for all speakers, and for younger speakers in Bury, Harwich, Ipswich, Woodbridge, and Hadleigh.
(c) The complete merger of /ʊ/ and /u:/, and of /ɒ/ and /ou/ before /l/, as in *pull:pool, doll:dole*, has taken place in Clacton and Walton, as well as in the speech of people under 30 or so in Colchester, Wivenhoe, and Felixstowe, and is variably present in younger Sudbury speech.
(d) Complete vocalization of /l/ has occurred only in Clacton, and there only for some speakers.

If, then, we wish to ascribe diffusion to accommodation, we would like to be in a position to argue that vocalization of [ɫ] is for East Anglians a salient feature of London and Home Counties English. It is not in fact a linguistic feature that is often commented on overtly by teachers or anybody else. On the other hand, it *is* a feature which is widely imitated when non-Londoners are copying London English for humorous or other purposes. It does not, of course, in its early stages involve loss of surface phonemic contrasts, but in its later stages it certainly does, leading, as we have seen, to a complex series of neutralizations and the development of a whole new set of diphthongs. We cannot, therefore, be absolutely convinced that *l*-vocalization is a feature for which we would have predicted accommodation, but there is at least some reason to suggest that the involvement of surface phonemic contrast does lead to a degree of salience. We can also argue for the phonological naturalness of this change, since the vocalization of dark *l* to an [u]-like vowel (and of clear *l* to [i]) is very well attested in the world's languages.

(2) The towns in the northern part of the East Anglian region – King's Lynn, Cromer, Dereham, Norwich, Great Yarmouth, and Lowestoft – have /au/ as in *house* as [æʉ]. All other towns have [ɛʉ] or [ɛu]. In the northern towns, the phonological process that Wells (1982) has labelled *smoothing*, whereby triphthongs consisting of diphthongs plus shwa become monophthongs, gives /au/ + /ə/ > [ɐ:], as in *tower* [tɐ:], *ploughing* [plɐ:n]. In middle-class accents, this vowel is identical

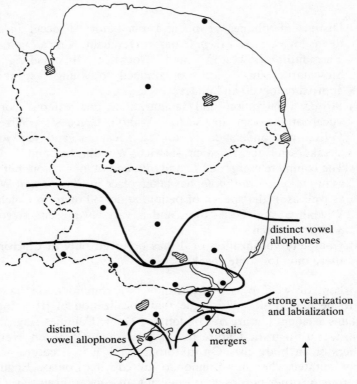

Map 2.3 /l/, older speakers, East Anglia

with the /ɑ:/ of *arm*, *path*, making *tower* and *tar* homophonous. Working-class accents, on the other hand, have /ɑ:/ as [a:], and therefore retain a distinction between *tar* and *tower* even when smoothing has taken place.

In fact, in these northern East Anglian towns, smoothing is perhaps more widespread than anywhere else in England, involving not only [ɑ:] in *tower* and [a:] in *fire*, but also producing *player* as [plæ:], *going* as [gɔ:n], *seeing* as [sɛ:n], *lower* as [lɒ:], and *doing* as [dɜ:n]. It is probably also part of a wider process that deletes post-vocalic /ə/, as in *there* [ðɛə] > [ðɛ:], *sure* [šʉə] > [šɜ:].

As map 2.5 shows, the smoothing of /ɑuə/ to /ɑ:/ and of other triphthongs is the only example the East Anglian study threw up of a linguistic change in progress that is spreading in a southerly rather than northerly direction: while older speakers in Ipswich, Woodbridge, Stowmarket, and Hadleigh have *tower* [tɛʉə] etc., younger speakers variably have the monophthongal forms, especially in the lexical set of *fire* and of *sure* and *there*. This diffusion of a linguistic innovation in the

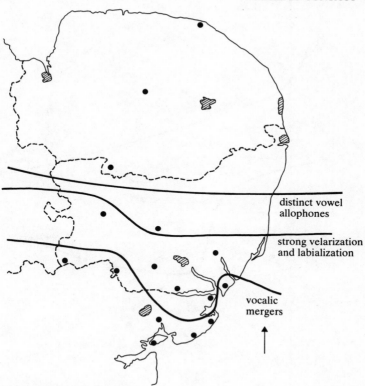

distinct vowel
allophones

strong velarization
and labialization

vocalic
mergers

Map 2.4   /l/, younger speakers, East Anglia

'wrong' direction poses some problems for an explanation based on a diffusion model that incorporates distance and population parameters. It is these models that tell us to expect the state of affairs that we most often find with respect to geographical diffusion in East Anglia, namely that forms spread out from London, which is broadly speaking to say from south to north. It is not, in fact, yet clear why smoothing is spreading southwards, but it is likely that we will be able to seek an explanation in the fact that smoothing already occurs not only in Norwich, for example, but also with certain vowels in London, in the midlands, and in the RP accent. Geographically, smoothing may have originated in a number of different locations.

Whether smoothing, again, can be assigned a high degree of salience such that we would predict that it would be accommodated to, and therefore diffused geographically, is not clear. Again, it is not a feature that appears to attract much overt comment. On the other hand, it is probable that in Norwich English at least it is a linguistic variable of the marker type. And once again it certainly does involve surface phonemic

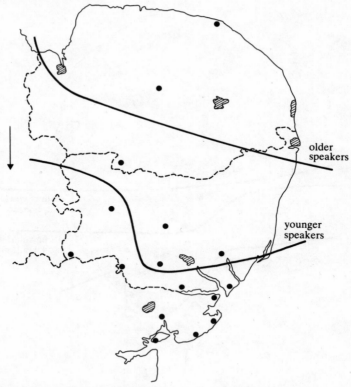

Map 2.5   Monophthongization of /ɑuə/ etc., East Anglia

contrasts, since we get, in northern East Anglia, the following equivalences:

tower	/ɑu/ + /ə/ > /ɑː/	as in *tar*
fire	/ɑi/ + /ə/ > /ɑː/	as in *far*
do it	/ʉː/ + /ə/ > /ɜː/	as in *dirt*
pure	/ʉə/ > /ɜː/	as in *purr*
going	/uː/ + /ə/ > /ɔː/	as in *lawn*

(3) The boundary between East Anglia, which has /ʌ/ and /ʊ/ distinct, as in *cud* and *could*, and the midlands, which in vernacular speech has only /ʊ/, runs to the west of King's Lynn through the Fenland, close to the Norfolk–Lincolnshire border (see Chambers and Trudgill, 1980). Nevertheless, in our East Anglian data there is a clear phonetic gradient in the actual realization of the /ʌ/ vowel (see figure 2.1; map 2.6). Wisbech has [ɣ], and King's Lynn [ə], while older rural Norfolk speakers in most of the county have the back vowel [ʌ] (i.e. unrounded [ɔ]).

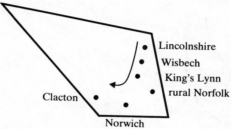

Figure 2.1   /ʌ/ in East Anglia

Norwich, Cromer, Dereham, Great Yarmouth, Lowestoft, and Stow-market all have an RP-like central [ɐ] for all age groups. The other urban centres in the south of the region, however, are undergoing change in the realization of /ʌ/, in that the fronting of this vowel, which is typical of London and Home Counties speech, is on the increase. These towns, that is, have vowel qualities for /ʌ/ ranging from [ɐ] to [a̠] depending on the age of the speaker and the proximity of the town to London.

This is a serious problem for the approach we have been adopting. We have no evidence that front realizations of /ʌ/ are particularly salient for East Anglian speakers, and there seems to be no particular reason why they should be. The change is a gradual and phonetic one, with no phonemic oppositions involved. And the phonetic distance between the different regional variants would not appear to be sufficient to draw attention to this vowel. Yet, the evidence is clear that diffusion is taking place. We are forced, therefore, to take the position that in this case a non-salient feature is being diffused and therefore, we assume, being accommodated to, as more northerly East Anglian speakers come into contact with more southern speakers. If this is the case, then it may be that the explanation for the success of this fronting of /ʌ/ may lie in an *accelerating* factor alone, namely that of phonological naturalness – in this case of the chain-shift type, having to do with pressures in phono-logical space (Martinet, 1955) (see figure 2.2). That is, the same impetus that led to the beginnings of this change in London itself is sufficiently strong to encourage its spread geographically also.

Nevertheless, we must concede that any initial optimism about our ability to predict precisely which linguistic features will be diffused from one variety to another is a little dampened by the phenomenon of the fronting of /ʌ/ in East Anglia. It is therefore comforting to note that the principles that we adopted in chapter 1 are of some considerable value when we come to an examination of those London features which *could* have been diffused out into East Anglia but which, so far at least, actually have not been.

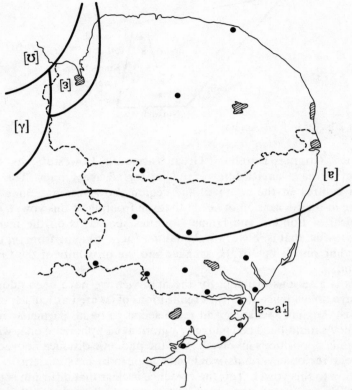

Map 2.6   /ʌ/ in East Anglia.

We noted above that in southern East Anglia younger urban speakers 'sound like' Londoners, but that closer linguistic analysis shows that they do preserve a number of non-London, East Anglian features. These features include:

(a) /ɑː/ in *far* etc. as [aː] rather than [ɑː] (see also chapter 4, p. 136)
(b) /iː/ in *meat* as [ɪi] rather than [əɪ]

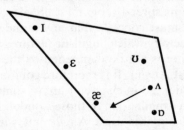

Figure 2.2   Phonological pressures leading to /ʌ/ fronting

(c) /ə/ in *water* as [ə] rather than [ɐ]

(d) /ə/ in *horses, wanted* etc. rather than /ɪ/ (see also chapter 4, p. 135).

These features constitute, for the linguist, striking differences between London and East Anglian phonology. They are, on the other hand, very slow indeed to diffuse into East Anglia, if indeed they diffuse at all. Note, therefore, that feature (a) is a purely phonetic difference that we would not expect to be salient, and that it is the same feature that we saw in chapter 1 to be not even accommodated to *within* a single speech community. Feature (b) is similarly a purely phonetic difference of very low salience. Features (c) and (d) both involve unstressed syllables but could be argued to be of some potential salience, since in feature (c) London [ɐ] is identical to East Anglian /ʌ/, while in feature (d) alternation between two phonemes is involved – normally a sure sign that a difference will be salient. It is therefore gratifying to note that in both cases we can point to the presence of the same strong inhibiting factor we noted in the case of accommodation in chapter 1: phonotactic constraints. If London [ɐ] is indeed identified with East Anglian /ʌ/, it can nevertheless not be transmitted as such into East Anglian English since /ʌ/, one of the checked vowels that occurs in closed syllables only, obviously cannot occur in word-final position. And unstressed /ɪ/ is unlikely, for many East Anglian speakers, to replace /ə/ in items such as *horses* and *wanted* since their accents have a phonotactic rule which allows /ə/ as the only vowel which may occur pre-consonantally in unstressed syllables. Thus *David* /ˈdæivəd/~/ˈdeːvəd/, *village* /ˈvɪləj/ etc. Indeed, conservative East Anglian accents, at least in the north of the region, have a rule which permits /ə/ as the only unstressed vowel in *any* unstressed syllable, including word-final position:

money	/mˈʌnə/
very	/vˈɛrə/
window	/wˈɪndə/
Tuesday	/tˈʉːzdə/ etc.

Phonotactic constraints may change of course, as they have in more innovating East Anglian accents, which now permit final -/iː/ in *money* etc. and -/uː/ in *window* etc. But in the meantime they may have a very inhibiting effect on accommodation to other dialects and, as a consequence, on the process of diffusion.

Diffusion through accommodation: a problem

There is still one feature subject to diffusion into East Anglia from London that we have not yet discussed. This is the variable merger of /θ/

with /f/, and of /ð/ with /d/ (word-initially) and /v/ (elsewhere), which is a well-known feature of London English (see Wells, 1982). In the East Anglian study, these mergers provide a striking and challenging example of the geographical spread of linguistic innovations. In the speech of informants in the region aged over 30, these mergers are not found at all anywhere, except for a small number of speakers in Clacton. In the speech of informants aged under 25, on the other hand, and most strikingly in the speech of teenage informants, we find these mergers in the accents of *all* the urban centres except Dereham, Cromer, and King's Lynn. It is, however, for most speakers a very variable feature, and is much more common with /θ/ than with /ð/. (It is also relatively unusual in the speech of middle-class informants.)

The extraordinarily rapid geographical diffusion of this particular linguistic feature is one that requires examination and explanation. Our data show that the merger is totally absent from the speech of even 11-year-olds in the 1968 Norwich survey, but that it is very common indeed in the speech of working-class 16-year-olds in the 1983 Norwich survey. That is, speakers born in 1957 do not have it at all, while speakers born in 1967 have it extensively (see map 2.7). The problem then is this. If we are claiming that accommodation is crucial to the geographical diffusion of linguistic innovations, and if we are also claiming that face-to-face interaction is essential for accommodation to take place, then how do we explain the prevalence of this merger in Norwich *adolescent* speech? The London-based innovation is making its way into Norwich and other East Anglian centres, but it is found for the most part in the speech of exactly those people who, probably, have least face-to-face contact with Londoners – namely teenagers. We have no figures for face-to-face contacts, but it does seem likely that conversations with the working-class Londoners who have this merger are most often carried out by *adult* working-class Norwich people who travel to the London area or meet Londoners in the course of their work.

A number of explanations, all of them speculative, can be advanced for this phenomenon. For instance, we can argue for the importance of attitudinal factors, and claim that the desirability of Cockney for adolescent males, with its stereotyped image of street-sophisticated toughness, is more important here than accommodation in face-to-face contact. (Casual observers have in fact argued here for the impact of television programmes such as the very popular 'Minder' in which the main characters speak Cockney. If this were the *only* influence, however, we would expect to find /θ/ being merged with /f/ all over Britain. This is definitely not what we do find. Rather we find a clear pattern of geographical spread, with towns nearer to London being influenced

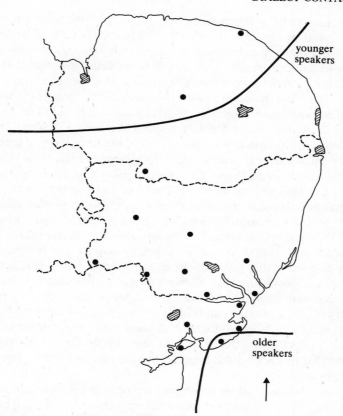

Map 2.7   Merger of /θ/ and /f/, East Anglia

before those further away, and those even further away not being influenced at all. Television *may* be part of a 'softening-up' process leading to the adoption of the merger, but it does not *cause* it.) We can also argue, instead or as well, that face-to-face contacts do take place, but perhaps in Norwich rather than in London, with tourists, in-migrants or even visiting football supporters bringing new linguistic forms in with them. One can even argue that the spread of the loss of the /f/–/θ/ contrast might be due to an increasing failure by adults in Norwich to correct /f/ for /θ/ as an infantilism. This in turn would be due to increasing familiarity with – and therefore increased tolerance of – this London feature on the part of adults as a result of *their* face-to-face contacts with Londoners.

However, it seems unlikely that any of these factors on their own can seriously be advanced as the major explanation. In particular, tourists in

Norwich tend to be of the middle-class, cathedral-visiting, /θ/-pronouncing type, and in any case the threshold hypothesis that we developed above suggests that occasional contacts with temporary visitors are unlikely to have any strong influence. It is possible, however, that some or all of these factors in combination may be of some relevance.

There are also, however, two other potentially important ways in which East Anglian teenagers might have extended face-to-face contacts with speakers of London English without themselves actually leaving their own area. In both cases, the bearers of the London-type forms are in a very small minority, and so we must assume considerable influence from attitudinal factors; but at least we can point to genuine face-to-face contact, and thus accommodation. First, we can recall from chapter 1 that it has now become clear that there may be speakers who have lived all their lives in a particular area who have failed, at some points, to acquire the local accent correctly. We saw that Norwich speakers whose parents are not natives of the area fail to acquire the normal *moan –mown* distinction that the majority of local people have. This of course opens up the possibility that Norwich English will eventually lose this distinction, not only as a result of accommodation by speakers to speakers of RP, London, and other external forms of English, but also through accommodation to these 'fifth columnists' who appear to speak the local dialect, but who in fact do not exactly do so. We have no evidence that this is what has happened in the case of *fin–thin*, but it is at least a possibility.

Secondly, we can look at another group of individuals who may have an influence out of all proportion to their percentage in the population. The American linguist and dialectologist Gary Underwood reports (personal communication) from his childhood in the rural American south that children who moved with their families to urban areas such as Memphis and then returned, say, two years later, having acquired the urban dialect, were very influential in spreading urban speech forms to their rural friends. These individuals were known and considered still to be locals, insiders. Their language was therefore not ignored or rejected as being foreign and alien as it would have been had they been genuine outsiders. They were therefore accommodated to, particularly since they were felt to be more sophisticated than the stay-at-homes. The same point is made by the pioneering Norwegian social dialectologist Anders Steinsholt. In his study of the dialect of Hedrum, southern Norway, and the influence on it of the dialect of the neighbouring town of Larvik, Steinsholt (1962) develops the notion of the *språkmisjonær* or 'language missionary'. He writes (my translation):

> The urban dialect spreads into Hedrum partly as a result of the influence of particular individuals living in different parts of the

area. Such individuals – we can call them 'language missionaries' – may be village people who have been particularly heavily influenced by the urban dialect. The most important language missionaries are first the young girls who come home after living for a while in the town, and secondly the whalers.

Factors such as these cannot be incorporated readily into explanatory diffusion models. They do nevertheless stress the importance of linguistic accommodation in the diffusion process. If the attitudinal factors are right, and particularly if individuals are perceived as being insiders by a certain group of speakers even though they are linguistically distinct, then they can have a considerable linguistic influence through face-to-face contact in spite of being heavily outnumbered. This is to say that, while a number of different factors have probably been at work in bringing about the dramatic introduction of the /f/–/θ/ merger to Norwich (and other centres), a very important feature may well have been the in-migration of a relatively small number of families and individuals into the city from the London area, and the return to Norwich of families temporarily resident in this same area. Certainly, in-migration from the Home Counties to Norfolk has been heavy in the past 25 years.

The /f/–/θ/ mergers are also, of course, not at all surprising from the perspective of salience and accommodation. The mergers, obviously, involve a loss of contrast between phonemic units (with orthography perhaps having some influence), and as such must be highly salient. There is, it is true, some possibility of delay due to the inhibiting influence of homonymic clash, but the functional load in English of /θ/ and /ð/ is rather low (see Gimson, 1980), and minimal pairs such as *thin:fin, lather:lava* are rather hard to come by. And set against that there is the considerable accelerating influence of the high degree of naturalness of the loss of /θ/ and /ð/. Both are, of course, unusual in the world's languages, acquired late by children, and subject to loss or change in many varieties of English. They are phonologically marked, and good candidates for variable merger and eventual loss.

Partial accommodation in contact situations

We have been arguing, then, that accommodation, with its constraints and therefore its regularities, is an essential part of the geographical diffusion of at least phonological forms. For a complete understanding, however, of what happens in contact between dialects, it is necessary to notice an important complication. This is that the linguistic form which is, as it were, transmitted from the originating dialect, is not necessarily identical to the form that is eventually acquired by the receiving dialect. There may well be, that is, a certain amount of disturbance during the transmission, presumably because of different types of 'imperfection' in accommodation. Some of these 'imperfections' may well simply consist in *incompleteness*, bearing in mind that speakers during accommodation reduce dissimilarities with other speakers, not imitate them slavishly.

One form of incomplete accommodation involves features from a contact dialect being *variably* acquired. This is what we saw happening with most of the features we discussed in chapter 1. Shockey's informants, for instance, have acquired [d] rather than [d̪] as a realization of intervocalic /d/, but they have not *lost* [d̪]. Rather, both forms are now used variably, and it is *frequencies* that change over time, as accommodation proceeds.

A second, related form of incomplete accommodation involves lexical diffusion. To understand how this operates, it is necessary to observe that accommodation, for all its constraints and regularities, is usually a rather piecemeal kind of activity. It may well be, for instance, that some English people resident in the USA eventually replace the /ɒ/ of their original phonological systems with the American equivalent /ɑ/. This, however, will only be the case if and when the process goes to completion. The point is that during accommodation speakers do not modify their phonological systems, as such, so that they more closely resemble those of the speakers they are accommodating to. Rather, they modify their pronunciations of *particular words*, in the first instance, with some words being affected before others. Speakers' motivation, moreover, is *phonetic* rather than phonological: their purpose is to make individual words sound the same as when they are pronounced by speakers of the target variety.

This can readily be demonstrated by an examination of dialect boundaries and the geographical diffusion process. Note, for example, what typically happens where, say, a dialect area with a five-vowel system adjoins an area with a six-vowel system. In spite of what dialect maps often suggest, it is usually not the case that we will find a particular community with the five-vowel system and a neighbouring community with the six-vowel system. For example, as is well known (see above), northern English English accents have the following system of checked vowels:

pit	/ɪ/	/ʊ/	*put, but*
pet	/ɛ/	/ɔ/	*pot*
	pat	/a/	

while southern varieties have the six-vowel system:

pit	/ɪ/	/ʊ/	put
pet	/ɛ/	/ʌ/	but
pat	/æ/	/ɒ/	pot

Southern accents distinguish *could* and *cud*, *put* and *putt*. Northern accents do not, having /ʊ/ throughout.

Dialectological research by the Survey of English Dialects based at Leeds University (Orton et al., 1962–71), and by others (see Chambers and Trudgill, 1980), shows that while there are large areas of northern and southern England where the five- and six-vowel systems respectively are found, there is also a transition zone of some considerable size between the two where *intermediate varieties* occur. These are varieties which have the contrast between /ʊ/ and /ʌ/, *but only to a certain extent*. The southern six-vowel system is gradually spreading northwards, and in this transition zone (depending also on phonological environment, frequency of occurrence, formality of style, and so on) some speakers have transferred or are transferring *particular words* from the /ʊ/ pronunciation to the /ʌ/ pronunciation (see table 2.2). Dialects which are of this sort we can call *mixed dialects*. Clearly, the speakers of these dialects are not accommodating to the southern vowel system *as such*, but changing their pronunciations of individual lexical items.

Table 2.2 Transition in mixed dialects

	put	bull	push	but	up	cup	butter	love	come
Northern	ʊ	ʊ	ʊ	ʊ	ʊ	ʊ	ʊ	ʊ	ʊ
Mixed	ʊ	ʊ	ʊ	ʊ	ʊ	ʊ	ʊ/ʌ	ʌ	ʌ
	ʊ	ʊ	ʊ	ʊ	ʊ/ʌ	ʌ	ʌ	ʌ	ʌ
Southern	ʊ	ʊ	ʊ	ʌ	ʌ	ʌ	ʌ	ʌ	ʌ

Sources: Orton et al., 1962–71, and Chambers and Trudgill, 1980.

Notice that we would expect this change to be spreading northward rather slowly since, as we saw in chapter 1, the /ʌ/ vowel of southern accents is not especially salient for northern speakers because, for them, it is not involved in any phonological contrast. (The whole change, of course, consists of the *acquisition* of the relevant contrast.) We would therefore expect relatively little accommodation to occur, and hence relatively slow diffusion. On the other hand, the large phonetic distance between high back rounded /ʊ/ and low central unrounded /ʌ/ will, we would expect, make for a certain degree of salience, and explain why the isogloss continues to move northward to the extent it does.

The same sort of process, but in reverse, can be seen at work (see Trudgill, 1983) in the diffusion of the loss of the *moan:mown* contrast (see chapter 1) out from the London area into East Anglia. The contrast between pairs such as *nose:knows*, *sole:soul*, *road:rowed* is disappearing, and the way in which it is disappearing in some areas is a mirror image of the process illustrated in table 2.2. Working-class speakers in the southern part of East Anglia, as a result of contact with and (incomplete) accommodation to speakers of dialects which have the merger, are effecting the merger in their own speech by *transferring* words, individually, from the /u:/ set to the /ʌu/ set. Table 2.3 summarizes the type of diachronic process involved. Stages 2 and 3 represent mixed dialects. For further examples of the same phenomenon, see Milroy (1978).

Table 2.3   Transition by word transfer

	Stage 1	Stage 2	Stage 3	Stage 4
road	/u:/	/u:/	/u:/	/ʌu/
moan	/u:/	/u:/	/ʌu/	/ʌu/
boat	/u:/	/ʌu/	/ʌu/	/ʌu/
low	/ʌu/	/ʌu/	/ʌu/	/ʌu/
know	/ʌu/	/ʌu/	/ʌu/	/ʌu/
old	/ʌu/	/ʌu/	/ʌu/	/ʌu/

Sources: Orton et al., 1962–71, Chambers and Trudgill, 1980.

Intermediate forms

Mixed dialects are varieties where accommodation is taking place, but where it has not gone to completion. We note now, however, that there are other ways in which accommodation can also be partial. Mixed dialects are *lexically* partially accommodated. In other varieties which, following Chambers (see Chambers and Trudgill, 1980), we can call *fudged dialects*, the accommodation is incomplete by being partial *phonetically*. What is involved is the development in dialect contact of forms that are *phonetically intermediate* between those of the original and target dialects. Table 2.4, for example, shows the sort of situation that occurs in fudged dialects in the /ʊ/–/ʌ/ transition zone between northern and southern England, in which contact between varieties with the vowel /ʌ/ and varieties with only the vowel /ʊ/ have given rise to an intermediate vowel quality [ɤ].

Similarly, in the case of the East Anglian *moan:mown* merger, some speakers, particularly those in the north of the area who come from middle-class backgrounds and have face-to-face contacts with RP speakers, are completing the merger by a process of *approximation*, which again involves the development of phonetically intermediate

Table 2.4 Transition in fudged dialects

	put	bull	push	but	up	cup	butter	love	come
Northern	ʊ	ʊ	ʊ	ʊ	ʊ	ʊ	ʊ	ʊ	ʊ
Fudged ⎧	ɤ	ɤ	ɤ	ɤ	ɤ	ɤ	ɤ	ɤ	ɤ
⎩	ʊ	ʊ	ʊ	ʊ	ɤ	ɤ	ɤ	ɤ	ʌ
Southern	ʊ	ʊ	ʊ	ʌ	ʌ	ʌ	ʌ	ʌ	ʌ

Source: Chambers and Trudgill, 1980.

forms. The /u:/ vowel and the /ʌu/ vowel are both gradually modified phonetically until they meet, as in table 2.5. (In the first instance, as stage 2 shows, the forms produced may be intermediate between those of the original and target dialects: original [u:] > intermediate [ou] > target [əu], parallel to the [ʊ] > [ɤ] (> [ʌ]) case above. Ultimately, however, since this is a merger and not a split as in the /ʌ/–/ʊ/ case, the end result, if the process goes to completion, *may* also be a vowel intermediate between the original dialect's formerly distinct vowels.) Stages 2 and 3 are typical of *fudged dialects*. Note that fudged dialects force a redefinition of *lexical diffusion* which, in that it focuses on the spread of changes through the lexicon, is usually characterized (see Wang, 1969) as being 'phonetically sudden but lexically gradual'. Clearly, fudging is both phonetically *and* lexically gradual.

Table 2.5 Transition by approximation

	Stage 1	Stage 2	Stage 3	Stage 4
road	/u:/	[u:]	[ou]	/əu/
moan	/u:/	[ou]	[əu]	/əu/
boat	/u:/	[ou]	[əu]	/əu/
low	/ɐu/	[əu]	[əu]	/əu/
know	/ɐu/	[əu]	[əu]	/əu/
old	/ɐu/	[ɐu]	[əu]	/əu/

Source: Chambers and Trudgill, 1980.

In the East Anglian case, it is clear why the two different strategies of transfer and approximation are employed, and why the two different types of dialect – mixed and fudged – result. Middle-class East Anglian speakers are accommodating to other middle- or upper-class speakers, including those present in their own community, who already have RP or near-RP accents in which the vowel of *boat, low* etc. is in fact [əu] or something close to it. The working-class speakers in the south, on the other hand, are accommodating to other working-class speakers resident in geographically adjacent areas who, as is typical of the London region, have a vowel of the type [ɐu~æu] in *boat, low* etc. In both cases the end result is phonological: a merger of two formerly distinct vowels and, at least in the next generation of speakers, the reduction of the inventory of vowels by one. The impetus for the change is also phonological: accommodation takes place because this feature has to do with phonemic contrast and is therefore salient. But in both cases, the immediate motivation is phonetic – the acquisition of a pronunciation of a particular word (and, subsequently, an increasingly large group of words) phonetically similar to that of the target accent. This motivation will, of course, also be operative even in cases where no phonological change results: there are East Anglian accents, for instance, where /u:/ has changed to /ɵu/ in the set of *boat, road* etc. under the influence of RP or other varieties, but where /ʌu/ in *low, know* etc. is still distinct.

Accommodation, therefore, may be incomplete in three different ways. Speakers may reduce pronunciation dissimilarities with other speakers (a) by alternating their own variant of a form with that of the other speakers; (b) by using the other speakers' variant in some words but not others (transfer/mixed dialects); and (c) by using pronunciations intermediate between those of the two accents in contact (approximation/fudged dialects). Of course, all three may occur in conjunction with each other.

Interdialect

Incomplete accommodation of the third type – the development of phonetically intermediate forms – particularly where this occurs on a wide scale during diffusion, is an especially interesting phenomenon. We propose to regard intermediate forms of this type as an example of *interdialect*. We use the term interdialect in the manner of the term *interlanguage* (Selinker, 1972), which is now widely used in studies of second-language acquisition. The label 'interdialect' is intended to refer to situations where contact between two dialects leads to the development of forms that actually originally occurred in neither dialect. (Interdialect forms are obviously of importance in the process of new-dialect formation, which we shall discuss in chapter 3.)

Interdialect, however, is by no means confined to the development of vowel sounds that are phonetically intermediate. Imperfect accommodation may lead to the (temporary or permanent) development of forms that are intermediate in other ways. For instance, Larsen (1907) explains the development in Oslo Norwegian of the diphthong /øy/ in a number of words such as *brøyt* 'broke' where it has no historical justification, as a result of a compromise between forms stereotyped as upper-class, with the monophthong /ø:/, and forms stereotyped as peasantlike, with the diphthong /æu/. It is of course the case that /øy/ can be regarded as being phonetically intermediate between /ø:/ and /æʉ/, but this vowel did not *develop* as a result of (social) dialect contact. It was already in existence, in words such as /gøy/ 'fun'. What happened was simply that words were reallocated to this vowel that formerly had /ø:/ or /æʉ/, and the selection of this vowel took place because it was phonetically intermediate.

The label 'intermediate' can also be applied to interdialect word forms, such as those studied by Rekdal (1971; cited in Venås, 1982). Rekdal investigated long-term accommodation by speakers from Sunndal, Norway, to Oslo Norwegian, after residence in Oslo of from one to five years. She noted the occurrence of a number of 'hybrid' forms in the speech of her informants that are found in neither Oslo nor Sunndal Norwegian. Examples include:

	Sunndal	*Oslo*	*interdialect*
'to work'	/jub/	/jɔbə/	/jubə/
'the matches'	/fyʂʈikɔɲ/	/fyʂʈikənə/	/fyʂʈikan/

Developments of this sort have, of course, long been noted by dialect geographers as occurring in geographical dialect contact areas and resulting in permanent interdialect forms in transition zones. At the lexical level, for instance, there is the well-known German dialect example where an area in which 'potato' is *Grundbirne* 'ground pear' is separated from an area where it is *Erdapfel* 'earth apple' by an intervening area in which the form is *Erdbirne*. A modern British example of the same phenomenon is the usage of *take away* in central and southern England to refer to Chinese and other establishments from which hot food can be bought for consumption off the premises. This southern area of Britain is divided from a northern area (mostly Scotland and Northern Ireland), where the term *carry out* is used, by an intermediate area (part of northern England) in which the intermediate form *take out* is employed.

It is important to note, however, that interdialect forms, defined as forms arising out of dialect contact which do not occur in the original dialects that are or were in contact, do not necessarily have to be *intermediate* in any simple or straightforward way. In the complex series of interactions that may arise in dialect contact situations, interdialect forms may arise out of accommodation that is 'imperfect' in ways other than by simply being incomplete.

A good grammatical example of this type of accommodation is provided by Cheshire (1982) on the speech of working-class adolescents in Reading, England. She observes a confusing situation in her tape-recorded data with respect to present-tense forms of the verb *do*: one finds in her data not only *I do* and *he does*, as in standard English, but also *I does* and *he do*, as well as *I dos* and *he dos* (/du:z/). It does not appear possible to correlate these forms satisfactorily with any social factors. Cheshire notes, however, that it is sensible to recognize that *do* is in fact two verbs in English, the main verb and the auxiliary. The same is true, of course, of *have*. In Reading English, the non-standard form *has* is used with all persons of the verb, and indeed, as in many other south-western dialects, the local dialect has *-s* as the marker of the present tense throughout the paradigm for all verbs: *I has, we goes, they likes* etc. Note, however, the percentage of non-standard *has* employed by the three groups of teenagers Cheshire investigated when tokens of *have* are divided into auxiliary and main verb:

percentage non-standard 'has'

	main verb	auxiliary
group A	43	0
group B	100	0
group C	52	0

The form *has*, that is, is only used for the full verb *have*. Where *have* is the auxiliary, forms without *-s* occur: *We has a good time* vs. *We've done it*. The same thing turns out to be true, although in a rather more complicated way, of *do*. If we distinguish between main verb and auxiliary categories, and also look separately at scores for third-person singular, which behaves irregularly in standard English, then Cheshire's data gives us the percentage of *do*, *does*, and *dos* forms given in table 2.6.

Table 2.6   Forms of *do* in Reading English (per cent)

	Main verb			Auxiliary		
	do	*dos*	*does*	*do*	*dos*	*does*
1, 2, 3 plural	36‡	*7	†57	*99‡	0	1
3 singular	14	*43	†43‡	*68	0	32‡

Source: Cheshire, 1982.

We interpret the figures in table 2.6 as follows. The original Reading dialect (and indeed this is confirmed by observations of the speech of elderly Reading speakers) distinguished between *do* for all persons as the auxiliary and *dos* for all persons as the main verb: the forms labelled * are the original dialect forms. The next stage, represented in the table by the sign †, involved the replacement of the dialect form *dos* by the standard English form *does*. Note, however, that we assume at this stage merely the importation of standard *forms*, not function: the distinction remained one between auxiliary and main verb, and not one between third-person singular and other persons. Now the final stage of the process involves the importation from standard English of this person distinction: standard English forms are signalled in the table by the sign ‡. Note that auxiliary *dos*, which occurs in neither the original Reading dialect nor standard English, scores 0 per cent. Note also that first-, second-, and third-person plural auxiliary *do*, which occurred in both dialects, scores 99 per cent, while third-person singular main verb *does*, when combined with the similar forms *dos* in the same context, scores 86 per cent. The other standard forms – first-, second-, and third-person plural main verb *do* (36 per cent) and third-person singular auxiliary *does* (32 per cent) – are doing quite well, but non-standard dialect forms are doing even better: first-, second-, and third-person plural main verb *does* at 57 per cent, and third-person singular auxiliary *do* at 68 per cent, although the former, as a result of standard influence, has almost replaced the original form *dos* (7 per cent). Finally, the 1 per cent figure under first-, second-, and third-person plural auxiliary *does* is probably so low as to be impossible to discuss with any confidence. What, however, of the figure of 14 per cent under third-person singular main verb *do*? This is a real puzzle because, while it does not occur in either of the two original dialects, it is nevertheless used 14 times out of every 100 by young Reading speakers, thus:

standard English	*original Reading*	*younger Reading*
I do it, do I?	I dos/does it, do I?	I does/do it, do I?
He does it, does he?	He dos/does it, do he?	He do/dos/does it, do/does he?

It can be argued, I believe, that the form *he do it* has developed and occurs as an *interdialect* form. It is a form that occurs in neither the original Reading dialect nor in standard English, but arises out of interaction *between* them. It is not really, of course, a fudged or an intermediate form, but it is a form that has arisen out of dialect contact. The mechanism is presumably hypercorrection or some other form of hyperadaptation (see below), but straightforward confusion in a rather complex situation – involving three forms, only one of which does not occur in the standard, and a switch-over from an auxiliary/main verb distinction to a person distinction – cannot altogether be ruled out. In any case, the main lesson we can draw from this – and it is an important one, since we shall be dealing in later chapters with dialect mixtures where more than two contact varieties are involved and where genuinely intermediate forms are therefore less likely – is that dialect contact via accommodation, with or without diffusion, is a complex process. We must be alert to *interaction* among dialects, rather than straightforward *influence*, as being instrumental in the development of interdialect.

Hyperdialectisms

Given that interdialect forms can arise out of interaction, as well as compromise, between dialects, we may now note further examples of interaction of different types, and at different linguistic levels. The example from the grammar of Reading English that we have just been discussing involved contact between social dialects, and the social diffusion of linguistic forms through accommodation. Equally interesting are similar interdialect forms that have arisen out of the *geographical* diffusion of linguistic features of the sort we discussed earlier in this chapter.

If we think about this type of diffusion in military terms, as it is often tempting to do, then it is perhaps not too fanciful to say that many urban centres in the south of England are, as it were, under attack linguistically from London. Our recent research in Norwich (see above) has demonstrated quite clearly that London-based forms such as the merger of /f/ and /θ/ are making their way into the English spoken there. It also shows, however, that in this state of siege a number of speakers of Norwich English appear to be actively engaged in fighting back. They are mostly younger working-class men, and the form their action against Home Counties and London incursions takes is an interesting one for historical linguistics and the study of linguistic change generally.

We can perhaps best describe the form that this linguistic rearguard action is taking by the label *hyperdialectism*. Hyperdialectism is a form of *hyperadaptation*, the best-known form of which is, of course, *hypercorrection*. Hypercorrections consist of attempts to adopt a more prestigious variety of speech which, through overgeneralization, leads to the production of forms which do not occur in the target prestige variety. A well-known British example of this is provided by north of England speakers' attempts to acquire a south of England pronunciation:

'correction' /bʊt/ > /bʌt/ *but*
hypercorrection /bʊčə/ > /bʌčə/ *butcher*

In an important paper, Knowles (1978) has pointed out that hypercorrection (and this will in fact be true of any form of hyperadaptation) is of two different types. In the first type, speakers perpetrate hypercorrections because, as it were, they do not know any better: their analyses of the target variety are faulty. In the second, speakers do have a correct analysis of the target variety, but they make mistakes 'in the heat of the moment' as performance errors which they may notice and may correct. In the flow of connected speech, they apply a conversion rule in an incorrect environment. Knowles points out that this is particularly likely to happen where two tokens of a segment that is a candidate for change occur in close proximity, but where only one of them should be changed. In the case of north of England to south of England adaptations, examples might include:

	north	south	hypercorrect
gas-mask	/gæsmæsk/	/gæsmɑːsk/	/gɑːsmɑːsk/
cup-hook	/kʊphʊk/	/kʌphʊk/	/kʌphʌk/

and of course forms such as /gɑːsmæsk/ and /kʊphʌk/ may also occur.

The hyperdialectisms that we are dealing with here all appear, importantly, to be of the first, misanalysis, type. The form that the hyperdialectism takes in Norwich is as follows. Parallel to the contrast between East Anglian /uː/ moan and /ʌu/ mown (see above), older varieties of East Anglian English also preserve the original Middle English ā and ai monophthong/diphthong contrast as in, for example:

$$daze \text{ /deːz/} = \text{[deɨːz]}$$
$$days \text{ /dæiz/} = \text{[dæɪz]}$$

That is, words such as face, gate, plate, mane, made etc. have /eː/, while words such as play, way, plain, main, maid etc. have /æi/. The loss of this distinction in East Anglia predates the loss of the /uː/–/ʌu/ distinction considerably, and in Norwich in 1968 (see Trudgill, 1974) it was a distinction that was retained only vestigially, and especially by older speakers, although most natives of the city were familiar with the pronunciation. Indeed, Kökeritz (1932) pointed out that, of the rural Suffolk localities he investigated, the dialect 'as spoken by elderly people, clearly distinguishes between words such as name (pronounced with [ẹː] and nail [pronounced with [æɪ] or [ɛɪ] which in standard English are pronounced alike' (p. 55), but he also pointed out that this distinction, even then, was dying out under the influence of RP and Cockney, with younger people generalizing [æɪ~ɛɪ~eɪ] to both groups of items. Similarly, in the records made by the American dialectologist Guy Lowman in the 1930s (see Trudgill, 1974), a vowel of the type [æɨ] is found throughout Norfolk and Suffolk in eight, pail, they, way, while a vowel of the type [e·ə~ɛə~ɛe] occurs in paper, lane, apron, make etc. However, the word chamber has [æɨ] rather than [e·ə] in most of the localities, and in the Suffolk village of Martlesham the words bracelet, relations, make, apron all have [æɨ~ɛɨ] alternating with [e·ə], which is labelled as 'older'. The 1950s Survey of English Dialects Norfolk records, made by W. Nelson Francis (ms.), show many cases of the /æi/–/eː/ distinction preserved, but Francis writes in his notes under the village of Ludham that ME ā has 'several different variants, perhaps indicative of change – [ɛ~e] no longer than half-long with lax high off-glide – forms with [æɪ] may show phonemic shift with reflex of ME ai, ei'. The extent to which the /eː/ vowel had become a relic form in

Norwich in 1968 is indicated by the fact that it was used by only 11 out of 60 informants and that all of them were aged 45 or over.

In spite of this relatively low level of usage, however, I argued in my report on the 1968 survey (Trudgill, 1974) that native speakers of Norwich English nevertheless had distinct underlying vowels for the sets of *name* and *nail*, and/or that they had access to some form of community diasystem, which preserved this distinction. The evidence was, in part, that speakers who normally never made the distinction were able to do so, *without error*, if they wished to do so for humorous or other purposes. Indeed, during the 1968 survey, a number of younger informants who did not have the distinction were able to produce it, consistently and correctly, when asked to read aloud a passage as they thought older speakers would read it. This distinguished them from outsiders who, in imitating the local dialect, often introduced the distinctive /e:/ vowel into words where it did not belong. As far as local Norwich speakers were concerned, however, even if all speakers did not make the surface contrast, they did all have access in some sense to a common set of distinct underlying forms.

I am now persuaded (see Trudgill, 1983) that this 'community diasystem' view is in any case wrong. But it also appears that the situation in Norwich is now no longer what it was in 1968. It is now no longer necessarily the case that members of the local speech community can be distinguished from outsiders in their ability to differentiate between the two lexical sets. The fact is that a number of Norwich speakers – especially, as we saw above, younger working-class males – are now using the vowel /e:/ in the *wrong* lexical set, and employing pronunciations such as *day* /de:/ etc.

We can suppose a development as follows. Contact between dialects is leading to the dying out of original East Anglian forms in the face of invading London and standard forms. In this dialect death situation, younger speakers no longer acquire the correct, original, phonological vowel distinction. They nevertheless retain a knowledge of *phonetic* differences between the older local dialects. Favourable attitudes towards the old variety and/or unfavourable attitudes towards the new, invading variety lead to the maintenance of the older phonetic form and, crucially, its extension into words where it is not historically justified. Hyperdialectisms of the type *days* /de:z/ thus arise out of dialect *interaction*:

	London	Norwich
days	/dæɪz/	/dæiz/ ⇒ /de:z/
daze	/dæɪz/	/de:z/

The new forms occur in neither of the two dialects in contact, and yet arise out of their interaction one with the other. They are therefore *interdialect* forms.

A very early observation of interdialect forms of this hyperdialectism type comes from the work of the Norwegian dialectologist Amund B. Larsen, who must have been one of the first linguists in the world to have carried out research into urban dialects. His publications include *Kristiana Bymål* (the urban dialect of Christiana–Oslo) (1907) and, with other authors, *Bergens Bymål* (1911–12) and *Stavanger Bymål* (1925). In Larsen (1917) he develops the notion of *nabo-opposisjon*, literally 'neighbour opposition', to refer to a type of hyperdialectal phenomenon. He notes the following dialect forms in the speech of the inner Sogn area of Norway (see map 2.8):

	standard	
Sogn	Norwegian	
/bjɔrk/	/bjørk/	'birch'
/çɔt/	/çøt/	'meat'
/smɔr/	/smør/	'butter'

The Sogn forms are unusual, unexpected, and impossible to explain historically. Larsen explains their occurrence by pointing out that there are a large number of other words where Sogn dialect (and standard

Map 2.8   Sogn and Hallingdal. Norway

Norwegian) have /ɔ/ as a normal historical development, and where the neighbouring Halling dialect has the vowel /ø/ (a development which does have an historical explanation). We thus have the development:

	Halling	Sogn
birch	/bjørk/	/bjørk/ ⇒ /bjɔrk/
top	/tøp/	/tɔp/

The regularity of the /ø/–/ɔ/ correspondences between the Sogn and Halling dialects was so salient for Sogn speakers that they were led to introduce the vowel typical of Sogn, as opposed to Halling, even into lexical items where they did not belong. Interaction between two dialects led to the development of forms that did not originally occur in either of them.

Larsen's paper may be the first report of the phenomenon of hyperdialectism. Once one has become alerted to this phenomenon, however, it becomes apparent that it is probably a not uncommon consequence of certain sorts of dialect contact. I cite three more examples from recent work on dialects of English English.

(1) In south-western English and southern Welsh traditional dialects, there is an interesting aspectual distinction unknown in most other varieties of English. It is of the following type:

punctual	*habitual*
I went there last night.	I did go there every day.
I go to Bristol tomorrow	I do go there every week

In the habitual forms, the *did* and *do* are unstressed, and in fact the *do* is most often pronounced /də/. (Indeed, it is highly probable that this is the source of the /de~də/ habitual/progressive marker that is found in the English-based Atlantic Creoles.)

Ihalainen (1976) has shown that in the south-west of England, the habitual/punctual aspect distinction is best preserved in the speech of older dialect speakers. That is to say, very many middle-aged and younger speakers no longer make the distinction. We can, once again, assume dialect contact in which traditional south-western dialect forms are being replaced by forms from the south-east and/or from the standard. It is therefore interesting to observe that the recent research of Bert Weltens has shown (see Edwards et al., 1984) that non-standard past-tense forms of the type *I did see it every day* are still widely used by some groups of younger working-class speakers in the Somerset–Wiltshire area. Weltens (ms.) also found, however, that the same speakers are also using constructions such as *I did see it last night*. They are, that is, using the non-standard habitual forms with punctual meaning. The non-standard south-western grammatical form is retained in the face of competition from other dialects, but as a result of contact with these dialects the correct semantic distinction is no longer retained. The non-standard habitual form has been generalized, as a hyperdialectism, into contexts where the original dialect would have had punctual forms such as *I seen it last night*. It therefore seems likely that if the typical south-western forms with unstressed *do* and *did* survive, they may actually increase in frequency but at the expense of the loss of the traditional dialect distinction. Dialect contact will have led not to the loss of a particular dialect form, but to the loss of a grammatical distinction.

(2) Similarly, it is well known that many dialects of English have restored the singular–plural distinction in second-person pronouns. This distinction was lost when originally plural *you* was extended in polite usage to the singular and subsequently, except in a number of rural dialects in Britain, replaced *thou* altogether. Well-attested examples (see Francis, 1967) of plural second-person pronouns (contrasting with singular *you*) include *you-all*, *y'all* (southern USA); *you'uns*, *youseyins* (Scotland and elsewhere); *you . . . together* (East Anglia, e.g. Come you on together! = Come on!). Irish English in many of its varieties has a singular–plural distinction *you–youse* which is categorical for very many speakers. (Lesley Milroy, 1984 reports that she caused confusion by greeting a group of women in Belfast with *How are you?*) This *you–youse* distinction is not known in that form anywhere in Britain, except where it has been introduced through large-scale immigration from Ireland, such as in Glasgow and Liverpool. From the inner-city areas of Liverpool, however, it has now spread out into the surrounding areas of Merseyside, as have many other features of Liverpool English. In this dialect contact situation, however, it is apparent that hyperdialectal usage has become established. Newbrook (1982) reports that the non-standard, originally plural form *youse* is now widely used by speakers in the Merseyside area as a singular pronoun, as in *Hello John, how are youse?* A similar development appears to have taken place in parts of the USA (Keith Walters, personal communication) where *y'all* has become singular (as well as plural) for some speakers (although this has been disputed; see also Spencer, 1975). In both cases, the non-standard form is not only retained but extended into grammatical contexts where it does not belong as a result of dialect contact.

(3) In English accents around the world, a number of interesting phenomena occur concerning non-prevocalic /r/ – the /r/ in the lexical set of *cart*, *car* etc. Some of these phenomena are related to dialect contact, and some not. It is useful to distinguish between these different phenomena in as accurate a manner as possible.

As is well known, English accents fall into two main types with respect to this feature: the *non-rhotic* or '*r*-less' varieties, which do not have non-prevocalic /r/; and the *rhotic* or '*r*-ful' accents, which do (see Wells, 1982; and chapter 1).

The *non-rhotic* varieties demonstrate the following features:

(a) *Linking* /r   This is not found in some varieties of South African and Black American English, but is normal in other *r*-less accents. Words such as *car* are pronounced without an /r/ except when followed by another word or morpheme beginning with a vowel. The /r/ which occurs in this environment is known as *linking* /r/.

(b) *Intrusive* /r/   Words such as *bra* are pronounced without an /r/ except when followed by another word or morpheme beginning with a vowel. The /r/ which occurs in this environment is known as *intrusive* /r/ – 'intrusive' because it is not 'historically justified' or present in the orthography. Most accents which have linking /r/ also have intrusive /r/, at least in some environments, but it is regarded as undesirable by some purists.

The development and occurrence of intrusive /r/ is normally explained in the following way. Non-rhotic accents are *r*-less because of a sound change, which appears to have begun in the south-east of England, in which /r/ was lost before a consonant, as in *cart*, or before a pause, as in *car*. In words where a vowel followed, such as *carry* and *rat*, the /r/ remained. As a consequence, words such as *car*, where the original /r/ was word-final, actually acquired two pronunciations, one without an /r/, as in *new car, car port*, and one with an /r/, as in *car insurance*. The sound change

$$/r/ > \o / \_\_ \left\{ \begin{matrix} C \\ \# \end{matrix} \right.$$

thus led to alternating forms such as /kɑːr/ and /kɑː/, depending on the environment. This eventually became reinterpreted synchronically, by analogy, not as a rule deleting /r/ before a consonant, but rather as its mirror image – a rule *inserting* /r/ before a vowel:

$$\o > /r/ / \_\_ V$$

(where preceded by an appropriate vowel – see below). Words such as *bra* thereby also acquired two pronunciations – one with a final /r/, as in *bra advert*, and one without, as in *new bra* – and thus rhymed with *car* in all environments.

By the time this change took place, only a certain number of English vowels occurred before /r/, and thus the operation of the

intrusive /r/ and linking /r/ insertion rule (they are of course the
same rule, the terminological distinction being a purely diachronic and/or prescriptive one) is confined to environments following
those vowels. Indeed, south-eastern English English accents can
now be said to have four distinct vowel subsystems:

(i) Those which produce a following /r/ when word- or morpheme-final and when another vowel follows:

/ɪə/	as in	*beer*
/ɛə/		*bear*
/ɜ:/		*fur*
/ɑ:/		*car*
/ɔ:/		*for*
/ə/		*letter*

Only /ɪə/ as in *idea*; /ɑ:/ as in *bra, chacha-ing*; /ɔ:/ as in *law,
drawing*; and /ə/ as in *America, banana-ish* can be said to produce
intrusive /r/, since /ɛə/ and /ɜ:/ derive only from historical V + /r/.

(ii) Vowels which produce a following /w/ when word- or morpheme-final and another vowel follows:

/u:/	as in	*you*
/ou/		*know*
/au/		*how*

(iii) Vowels which produce a following /j/:

/i:/	as in	*me*
/ei/		*play*
/ɑi/		*lie*
/ɔi/		*boy*

(iv) Vowels which cannot occur word-finally – the 'checked'
vowels:

/ɪ/	as in	*pit*
/ɛ/		*pet*
/æ/		*pat*
/ʊ/		*put*
/ʌ/		*putt*
/ɒ/		*pot*

As we shall see below, this historical explanation for the development of intrusive /r/, while surely correct, may not be the whole
story.

(c) *Hyperadaptive* /r/   In those parts of the USA where the majority of the population are *r*-less but where rhotic accents are held to be prestigious, such as, increasingly, parts of eastern New England as well as in American Black English, non-prevocalic /r/ may occur in words where it does not 'belong', through hyper-correction. Similarly, English pop singers (see Trudgill, 1983) and actors imitating American accents (and indeed rhotic British and Irish accents) can also be heard to employ 'hyper-American /r/' in these same lexical sets. The environments in which this occurs are after the vowels listed in (b)(i) above (or their American equivalents) for linking and intrusive /r/, but also before a consonant, as in *dawn, bought, palm,* or before a pause, as in *law, America* etc. That is, Bostonians who say *Chinar and Japan* are employing an intrusive /r/ which is part of their native accent; while if they say *Japan and Chinar*, they are indulging in hypercorrection. Similarly, British actors imitating Americans by saying *dawn* /dɔːrn/ are perpetrating hyper-American /r/. Clearly, hyperadaptive /r/ is a dialect contact phenomenon.

The *rhotic* varieties of English, in their turn, demonstrate the following features:

(a) *Analogical* /r/   In the rhotic accents of, for example, the south-west of England, individual lexical items occur from time to time with non-prevocalic /r/ where no /r/ would be expected. This occurs with neologisms and proper names as a result of faulty analyses of correspondences between rhotic and non-rhotic varieties. For instance, the word *Dalek* from the BBC TV programme 'Dr Who' was frequently pronounced /daːrlɛk/ by children from the south-west of England who were familiar with the fact that RP and south-eastern /ɑː/ often corresponds to south-western /ɑːr/. (Similarly, *khaki* can be heard as /karki/ in both Canada and Northern Ireland.) This is again, clearly, a dialect contact phenomenon.

(b) *Phonotactic* /r/   In a number of south-western English cities, including Southampton and Portsmouth, words such as *banana,. vanilla, America* are pronounced with final /r/. This appears to be a phenomenon different from analogical /r/, since it is widespread and normal as an integral feature of literate adult speech and occurs in well-established lexical items. Moreover, it occurs only in word-final position. Neither is it to be confused with intrusive /r/, since phonotactic /r/ occurs pre-pausally and pre-consonantally. Note that it is regionally restricted even within the rhotic area. We discuss the origins of this feature below.

(c) *Hyperdialectal /r/*   We now return to the subject of hyperdialectisms. The Survey of English Dialects (SED) materials (Orton et
al., 1962–71) show a number of interesting occurrences of what is
obviously hyperdialectal /r/ in rhotic areas. This is particularly
clearly illustrated in a number of the maps in the *Linguistic Atlas
of England* (LAE) (Orton et al., 1978), one of which – the map
for *last* – is reproduced here as map 2.9. This shows clearly that
there is a small area of Shropshire where the pronunciation of the
word *last* in a number of localities is not the usual [læst], [last], or
[la:st], but [la:ɹst]. Map 2.10, the LAE map for *arm*, shows that
this same area of Shropshire, at the level of traditional rural
dialect, is right at the boundary between rhotic and non-rhotic
areas.

Again, we can assume that the mechanism that is at work here
is hyperadaptation. In the border dialect contact situation, local
speakers observe that their /a:r/ in items such as *arm* corresponds
to neighbouring non-rhotic /a:/. The *r*-ful pronunciation therefore
becomes a local dialect symbol, and the use of that pronunciation
a way of indicating dialect and local loyalty.

It is also important to observe that hyperdialectal /r/ is not
confined to Shropshire. The SED materials give transcriptions
such as

walk	[wɔːɹk]
calf	[kɔːɹf~kaːɹf]
straw	[stɹɔːɹ]
daughter	[daːɹtəɹ~dɔːɹtəɹ]

in other rhotic/non-rhotic border areas of Herefordshire, Mon-
mouthshire, Worcestershire, and to a lesser extent Oxfordshire,
Warwickshire, Berkshire, and Buckinghamshire. It is significant
that there are no such hyperdialectisms in the rhotic heartlands
such as Devon and Somerset.

Presumably the psychological mechanism involved here is the
same as that dealt with by Labov in his work on Martha's
Vineyard (1963). As is well known, Labov showed that those
Vineyarders who identified strongly with the island and wished to
remain there had more centralized realizations of the first elements of /ai/ and /au/, which were typical of the local dialect, than
speakers who did not so identify. The latter, on the contrary, had
more open first elements, typical of the mainland. It seemed
probable that loyal Vineyarders not only were not participating in
sound changes of the type [ɐɪ] > [aɪ], but also were actually
reversing them, as [ɐɪ] > [əɪ].

Map 2.9   *last* (from *Linguistic Atlas of England*, Orton et al., 1978)

We can regard hyperdialectal /r/ on the rhotic side of the rhotic/ non-rhotic border areas as a way of reacting to and resisting new, non-rhotic pronunciations, since it is obvious that throughout England rhotic pronunciations are receding quite rapidly in the face of non-rhotic. We can also regard them – since multiple causation is always likely in linguistic change – as a result of dialect contact leading to a *dialect death* process, with a consequent loss of knowledge by local people of how exactly the local dialect is spoken.

Similar developments are reported to have occurred (Keith Walters, personal communication) in rhotic/non-rhotic border areas in the United States, such as parts of North Carolina and Texas. In these areas, items such as *walk* and *daughter* may be

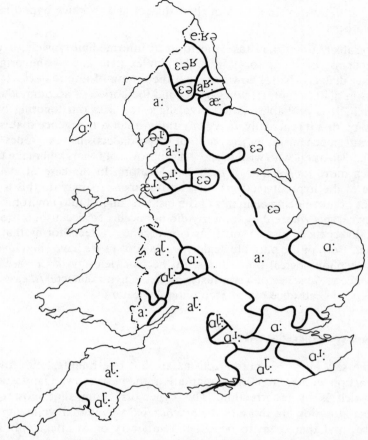

Map 2.10 *arm* (from *Linguistic Atlas of England*, Orton et al., 1978)

pronounced with /r/. In this case, however, we must note that in most areas of the USA rhotic pronunciations are more statusful than non-rhotic and are spreading at their expense. We cannot, therefore, adopt the 'reaction' explanation for the occurrence of this feature in the USA. It may, in fact, be an example either of hypercorrect /r/, or of hyperdialectal /r/, or of both. If it is hyperdialectal /r/, then it can be due only to the dialect death factor.

In any case, it is interesting to note that in England it is not just actors, pop singers, and other outsiders who misanalyse the occurrence of /r/ in rhotic accents. Local dialect speakers themselves, particularly if under attack from outside, may also overdo things in fighting back, and/or may lose track, in a dialect death

situation, of the rules of their dialect and produce hyperdialectisms.

Interdialect, then, may take the form of intermediate vowels, hyperdialectisms, or other forms that did not exist in any of the original
contact dialects. Note, however, that the notion of interdialect, as this
arises in dialect contact, takes us beyond the notion of accommodation
as such. It is probable, as we have suggested with our 'fighting back'
analogy, that it is actually *divergence* rather than convergence that is the
relevant mechanism in the case of hyperdialectisms. As Giles has
argued, speakers who wish to show disapproval of others will make their
speech more *unlike* that of their interlocutors. In the case of at least
some of the hyperdialectisms cited above, speakers may do this to the
extent of introducing elements of the insiders' dialect into environments
or lexical sets where they formerly did not occur. Notice also, however,
that divergence, just as much as convergence, affects forms that are
salient. Both of the phonological hyperdialectisms we have cited involve
surface phonological oppositions: in the Norwich *days:daze* case, the
presence vs. absence of a contrast; and in the hyperdialectal /r/ case, the
presence vs. absence of a shared phonological unit.

Long-term hyperadaptation

As we saw above, hyperdialectisms are but one manifestation of the
contact phenomenon of hyperadaptation, the best-known manifestation
of which is hypercorrection. The hypercorrections that most often
attract attention are those of the *butcher* /bʌčə/ type that we mentioned
above, and that seem to be either temporary or to affect only individuals. Occasionally, however, it is clear that hypercorrection gives rise
to large-scale linguistic change and results in interdialect forms becoming an integral part of a particular dialect. It is possible, for example,
that the midwestern USA pronunciation of *wash* etc. with /rš/ arose in
this way.

One such originally interdialect phenomenon in Britain is the 'Bristol
l', an accent feature which is well known to students of English English
accents (see Wells, 1982) and to many English people generally. The
term 'Bristol *l*' refers to the fact that in the working-class speech of the
major city of Bristol, and in certain immediately neighbouring rural
dialects, words such as *America, banana, idea* are pronounced with a
final /l/. That is, *ideal* and *idea, evil* and *Eva, normal* and *Norma, aerial*
and *area* are homophonous. This pronunciation feature is referred to in
a number of popular publications (e.g. Robinson, 1971). And the
Survey of English Dialects materials (Orton et al., 1962–71) show the

locality of Weston, Bath, Somerset (now Avon), near Bristol, as occasionally having [ɫ] after final /-ə/.

It is instructive to attempt to provide an explanation for the development of this feature. It is after all unusual and not repeated, to the best of my knowledge, anywhere else in the English-speaking world. (There are, it is true, similar features: speakers of the old Isle of Wight dialect have *drawling* for *drawing*, and some USA dialects have *I sawl it* rather than *I saw it* (Erik Fudge, Walter Pitts, personal communication); but these are linking, sandhi phenomena, whereas the Bristol *l* is not. The Bristol *l*, although confined to word-final position, does not depend on whether a consonant, vowel, or pause follows.) Although *l* loss and *l* vocalization are very well known indeed in the history of the world's languages, *l* addition is not common, to say the least.

A very plausible explanation for the historical addition of /l/ lies in hypercorrection. Wells (1982) writes:

> Intrusive /l/ is not a sandhi phenomenon: it can apply equally to a word which is sentence final or in isolation, and it varies allophonically between clear and dark according as the following segment is or is not a vowel. . . . Its origin must presumably lie in hypercorrection after the loss of final /l/ after /ə/, a hypothetical ['æpə] for *apple*. When the /l/ was restored under pressure from standard accents, it was added analogically to all words ending in [ə].

In other words, we have a scenario as follows:

	l loss	*correction*
evil	/iːvəl/ > /iːvə/	> /iːvəl/
Eva	/iːvə/	> /iːvəl/

This explains this somewhat peculiar development in terms of dialect contact and, perhaps, imperfect accommodation leading to an interdialect form.

There is, however, another factor which we ought to acknowledge. Observe, first, that it is possible to point to a number of difficulties with the hypercorrection explanation. One is, of course, that while a number of English varieties demonstrate /l/ loss, only Bristol has the Bristol /l/. Why is this? Another is that Bristol English does not have *law* */lɔːl/, *paw* */pɔːl/ after the pattern of *wall*, *pall*. It is perfectly possible, of course, for a variety to lose /l/ only in final unstressed syllables, but most varieties that have /l/ loss or vocalization do so in all syllable-final positions. Similarly, Bristol English does not have intrusive /l/ in items such as *medicine*, *cavity*, *finery* etc. after the pattern of *meddlesome*, *faculty*, *cavalry*, *hostelry* etc., where again one would *expect* – although this does not inevitably follow – *l* loss to occur if it were occurring word-finally in items such as *medal, tackle, ravel, hostel*. The facts are, however, that *medilcine, cavilty*, and *finelry* do not occur.

An additional factor that might account for this fact – that hypercorrection affected only word-final /ə/ – is a phonotactic one. Nearly all the words which have the Bristol /l/ in the Bristol accent are words ending orthographically in -*a*, and are relatively recent arrivals in English. Many of them are extremely recent, such as *Tanzania, Zambia, Coca Cola*. Others are relatively recent, such as *Canada, Arizona*. And even those which have been established in English for a few hundred years, such as *idea, India, China*, are medieval or post-medieval borrowings into English and not part of the indigenous Old English, Scandinavian, or French vocabulary. Now, as these words were being introduced into English and spreading from learned into general usage, it is probable that there was an area of south-eastern England where they were not phonotactically odd, since from the seventeenth century or so onwards varieties there had already lost final /r/ in words like *finer* /fainə/, so that new words like *China* /čainə/ were no problem. In other parts of the English-speaking world, however, where non-prevocalic /r/ had not been lost, such as western England, Scotland, and North America, words such as *China, Canada, America* must have been phonotactically odd, because there were no words in the indigenous vocabulary with final -/ə/#. Different rhotic varieties therefore adopted different methods of adapting these new words to their phonotactic structure, since, as we saw in chapter 1, phonotactic constraints may be powerful and difficult to overcome. Some of these methods are as follows:

(1) As we saw above, Wells has reported that some south-western English English dialects have converted these new words into an acceptable pattern by the addition of phonotactic /r/. A word like *China* is no longer phonotactically difficult because it is pronounced /čainər/. Similarly, there are many American varieties (in addition to those where *hypercorrect* /r/ occurs) where words such as *idea* are consistently pronounced with /r/ in all environments.

(2) There are also many varieties of English where word-final -*a* is realized as /i:/ or /ɪ/ as in *very, money*. For example, *soda* is commonly pronounced /soudi:/ in rural American dialects, and many other such words either still preserve -/i:/ in rural non-standard speech, or else formerly had such pronunciations, some of which are still preserved in songs and/or folk memory: *Virginny* = *Virginia, Ameriky* = *America*, and so on. Butters (1980) cites, in Appalachian dialects, *extry* = *extra, sofy* = *sofa, chiny* = *china*,

Nevady = *Nevada*. Similar pronunciations are also reported from Ireland.

(3) Scottish varieties of English, or at least some of them, are able to avoid this problem by employing the vowel of *pat* word-finally in these words. This is the result of the fact that all vowels in Scots English, with the exception of /ɪ/, /ɛ/, and /ʌ/, are able to occur in open syllables. There is, for example, no contrast between the lexical sets of *pull* and *pool*, with the result that the /u/ of *hood* can also occur in *who*. Similarly, there is no contrast between the sets of *cot* and *caught*, so that the /ɔ/ of *lot* can also occur in *law*. And, finally, there is no contrast between the vowels of the sets of *Pam* and *palm*, with the /a/ of *pat* occurring also in *pa*. Thus, words like *China* may end in -/a/, and words like *algebra* can begin and end with the same vowel (Milroy, 1981 on Belfast).

(4) Bristol English, in its turn, has accommodated the phonotactically uncomfortable loan words into its phonotactic system by the addition of final -/l/. Our argument is, in other words, that while the initial impetus for the development of the Bristol *l* was hypercorrection induced by dialect contact, this was reinforced – again noting the value of multiple causation as accounting for why a particular change, out of all possible changes, actually took place – by the addition over the years to the vocabulary of English of words that would, unmodified, have been phonotactically acceptable only in non-rhotic accents.

There are, of course, some difficulties with these explanations. We have, for example, no reasonable way of accounting for the fact that it is only Bristol English that has solved this problem in this particular way. And there are difficulties with widespread reports that Bristol English has final -/əl/ also in words such as *tango, window*. I have myself no evidence of this, and if these forms do occur they may be hyperdialect-isms. My data, taken from tapes supplied by Bristol Broadsides and employed by them in studies of local folk history, has older Bristol speakers employing word-final /l/ in *area, Eva, Australia, extra, idea, Victoria, cholera, gala, swastika* etc. There is, however, not a single occurrence of /l/ with items such as *window, barrow, calico, narrow, borrow, piano, widow, fellow, radio, tallow, beano, potato*. It is, how-ever, certainly the case that the name of the town itself used to be *Bristow*, from an earlier *Brycgstow* 'site of the bridge' (Ekwall, 1960). In spite of these difficulties, however, it is clear that any explanation for the development of the 'Bristol *l*' that did not look to some degree to the role of dialect contact would ignore what is obviously a major causal factor.

Conclusion

In this chapter, we have argued that linguistic accommodation to salient linguistic features in face-to-face interaction is crucial in the geographical diffusion of linguistic innovations. We have also shown that the diffusion of linguistic forms from one dialect to another may have a number of rather complex linguistic consequences, including the development of interdialect forms such as intermediate forms, hypercorrections, and hyperdialectisms. In the next chapter, we shall examine in more detail the way in which these developments are involved in the formation of new dialects in dialect contact.

3

Dialect Mixture and the Growth of New Dialects

We have just seen that dialect contact may lead to the development of interdialect forms, including intermediate forms. We have discussed this development in atomistic terms, noting how the process of partial accommodation may lead, in phonology, to alternation between variant pronunciations of the same vowel or consonant; to lexical diffusion; and/or to the growth of vowels or consonants that are phonetically intermediate between the variants in contact.

We now turn to a more holistic approach to dialect contact phenomena, in which we note that dialect mixture may give rise to whole new interdialectal *varieties* (or *interdialects*), including new intermediate dialects. It emerges that it is particularly rewarding to investigate this type of development in *divergent dialect* communities (see below) and in situations involving dialect transplantation, since in these cases the degree of dialect difference between the varieties involved tends to be greater than in straightforward geographical diffusion and contact in well-established areas, as discussed in chapter 2. This is because in the latter, as a result of perhaps centuries of diffusion, the dialects that are in contact tend to be very similar anyway, with little room therefore for whole new intermediate varieties to develop. We accordingly now begin to tackle the problem of *new-dialect formation* by concentrating on situations where transplantation of some form has occurred.

Language transplantation: Fronteiriço

One situation that makes the point about transplantation and new-dialect formation very clearly is that which is found in the Brazil–Uruguay border area. On the Iberian peninsula, as is well known, there is a geographical dialect continuum (see Matias, 1984; Kurath, 1972) where dialects of Catalan, Spanish, and Portuguese merge gradually into one another, and where the number of 'languages' recognized as being spoken depends on the number of autonomous, standard varieties that have succeeded in raising themselves above the dialect continuum. Speakers of dialects from the Catalan part of the continuum are generally, these days, regarded as speaking a language separate from Spanish/ Castilian, whereas the acceptance of Galician as a separate language is much more controversial.

In South America, on the other hand, the situation is very different. The Portuguese spoken in Brazil and the Spanish of those of Brazil's neighbours that are Spanish speaking do not merge into a dialect continuum. As varieties based originally on different, non-contiguous areas of the Iberian peninsula, Uruguayan Spanish and Brazilian Portuguese actually confront one another on the border between southern Brazil and northern Uruguay (see map 3.1). Here the two varieties of language meet – as they do not on the border of Spain and Portugal – in varieties which are related but which also have a considerable linguistic distance between them (although some degree of mutual intelligibility can be achieved), and which are normally acknowledged to be different languages.

There has therefore been linguistic 'room', as it were, for contact in this region to lead to the development of a new variety intermediate

Map 3.1   Fronteiriço

between the two. Hensey (1972, 1982) and other linguists such as Elizaincín (1973) and Rona (1963, 1965) have studied the region and described a widespread, complex, and somewhat institutionalized border situation involving contact and interaction between the two mutually intelligible varieties, which has in fact led in places to the growth of a (somewhat stable) intermediate variety or varieties. Hensey shows that in much of the border area, the Spanish of the Portuguese-speaking Brazilians tends to be weaker and less frequently employed than the Portuguese of Uruguayans. Very many, however, of both nationalities are bilingual to differing degrees, and many interference phenomena can be observed.

In the terms of Le Page and Tabouret-Keller (1985) there is clearly in most border areas a rather *diffuse* type of linguistic situation, but one which obviously has potential for *focusing*, since in some isolated northern Uruguayan areas there have grown up a number of different mixed varieties which are more Portuguese than Spanish but which have a very considerable Spanish element and which are spoken as the *sole* language of the communities in which they occur. These relatively more focused varieties, where they occur, are labelled (in the usage of Hensey and Rona) *fronteiriço/fronterizo*. (Other writers use this term for the more diffuse types of mixture also.)

According to Rona, characteristics of the (as we saw, mainly Portuguese) Fronteiriço include the reduction of the Portuguese seven-vowel system to a Spanish-style five-vowel system. And Hensey also indicates that, for instance, Portuguese /s/:/z/ are merged as /s/ in Fronteiriço, e.g. Portuguese /kaza/ 'house', Fronteiriço /kasa/; and Portuguese intervocalic /b d g/ are Fronteiriço /β ð ɣ], as in Spanish. An example sentence can convey something of the intermediate, interdialect nature of Fronteiriço:

>
> Portuguese: [todu u dzia]
> Fronteiriço: [tɔðu u ðia] 'all the day'
> Spanish: [tɔðɔ ɛl dia]

Focused and diffuse varieties

Le Page's terms *focused* and *diffuse* require some discussion. Le Page and Tabouret-Keller have pointed out (1985) that speech communities, and therefore language varieties, vary from the relatively focused to the relatively diffuse. The better-known European languages tend to be of the focused type: the language is felt to be clearly distinct from other languages; its 'boundaries' are clearly delineated; and members of the speech community show a high level of agreement as to what does and does not constitute 'the language'. In other parts of the world, however, this may not be so at all, and we may have instead a relatively diffuse situation: speakers may have no very clear idea about what language they are speaking; and what does and does not constitute the language will be perceived as an issue of no great importance.

This is particularly clear in what those of us from focused language backgrounds would tend to call multilingual situations. Le Page and Tabouret-Keller point out, for example, that in Belize most speech events can be conceived of as occurring at a particular location within a triangle of which the points are English, Creole, and Spanish (see figure 3.1). Belize is a relatively unfocused speech community, and speakers may at any time use different proportions of English, Creole, and Spanish. Some situations, it is true, may demand 'pure' English or Spanish, at or towards one of the points of the triangle. But many other situations do not make this requirement and may indeed require 'mixtures' of different proportions. Like other diffuse communities, moreover, Belize does have potentialities for focusing. It is not inconceivable, although currently it does not actually seem very likely, that social factors (such as Belizean nationalism) could lead to the development of a 'new' focused language variety, located somewhere in the triangle. If this variety were to acquire autonomy and a name of its own, it would come in time to be referred to as, say, 'Belizean', just as in England the medieval mixture of Old English, French, and Scandinavian elements came to be known as 'English'.

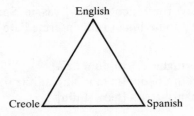

Figure 3.1   Speech events triangle for Belize

Social dialect continua: diffuse

In the same sort of way, dialect contact may give rise to both focused and diffuse types of language variety, as we noted in Brazil/Uruguay. One of the things that may happen in a *diffuse* situation is that two dialects in contact may give rise over time to a dialect continuum, with the original dialects remaining at either end. (Subsequently, focusing may take place around a particular point on this continuum, as we shall see below.)

One example of a diffuse, continuum-type situation is the well-known phenomenon of the *post-Creole continuum*. Some writers envisage the sort of scenario in figure 3.2 for the development of such continua: the acrolect, e.g. English, comes into contact with its related basilect, e.g. English Creole (stage A), which results in the growth of a whole series of intermediate mesolectal varieties (stage B) as well as in the convergence of the basilect on the acrolect (through the process of decreolization).

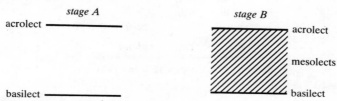

Figure 3.2   Post-Creole continuum

Perhaps the best known study of decreolization is Bickerton's work (1975) on the Guyanese post-Creole continuum. This concentrates on verb forms and discusses in considerable and interesting detail the processes through which two semantically and formally very different systems interact to produce intermediate forms.

Another such study is that of Cooper (1979, 1980), in which he deals with the linguistic situation on the Caribbean islands of St Kitts and Nevis (see map 3.2). As far as phonology is concerned, Cooper

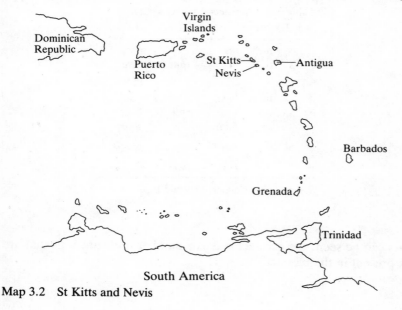

Map 3.2   St Kitts and Nevis

Table 3.1   Basilectal vowel system,
St Kitts-Nevis

i		u	*bit*		*foot*
e	ʌ	o	*bet*	*shut*	*owe*
	a			*pat*	
ii		uu	*beat*		*boot*
ia		ua	*wait*		*boat*
	aa			*bath*	
ai	ou		*bite*	*about*	

Sources: after Cooper, 1979 and 1980.

describes the basilectal St Kitts-Nevis vowel system as in table 3.1. The contrasting acrolectal vowel system is given in table 3.2. Note that the only major systemic differences between the acrolectal system and that of English English RP are (a) the presence of the extra vowel /o/ as in *owe*, and (b) the absence of any *fear–fair* distinction, both sets having /ie/ in the acrolect.

Table 3.2   Acrolectal vowel system,
St Kitts-Nevis

i		u	*bit*		*foot*
e	ʌ	o	*bet*	*shut*	*owe*
a		ɔ	*pat*		*pot*
ii		uu	*beat*		*boot*
ee	ʌʌ	oo	*wait*	*shirt*	*boat*
aa		ɔɔ	*bath*		*short*
ai	ɔi	ou	*bite*	*toy*	*about*
ie		ua	*fear*	*tour*	

Sources: after Cooper, 1979 and 1980.

As can be seen, the acrolect makes a number of distinctions that are not present in the basilect:

	acrolect	basilect
pot	/pɔt/	} /pat/
pat	/pat/	
fade	/feed/	} /fiad/
feared	/fied/	
shut	/šʌt/	} /šʌt/
shirt	/šʌʌt/	
toad	/tood/	} /tuad/
toured	/tuod/	
part	/paat/	} /paat/
port	/pɔɔt/	
toy	/tɔi/	} /tai/
tie	/tai/	

Note also that, just as the acrolect has *owe* with /o/, it also has *day* etc. with /e/ (rather than /ee/) and *two* etc. with /u/ (rather than /uu/). Items such as *lost*, *gone* have /ɔɔ/ (basilectal /aa/) rather than /ɔ/ (cf. older RP /lɔ:st/, /gɔ:n/, rather than modern /lɒst/, /gɒn/).

For our purposes, the interesting aspect of the St Kitts-Nevis continuum is the way in which interaction between the two polar varieties has given rise to intermediate, mesolectal varieties. Our observations in chapter 2 lead us to expect the development of a number of interdialect phenomena, as phonological distinctions are added higher up the continuum. If hypercorrections occur, for instance, they will obviously be of the form *pat* = /pɔt/ instead of /pat/, *cart* = /kɔɔt/ instead of /kaat/ etc.

Cooper does not in fact mention the occurrence of any hypercorrect forms, but he does show that some *intermediate* forms occur, as with the following:

	basilect	intermediate	acrolect	RP-type
face etc.	/fias/	/fies/	/fees/	/feis/
boat etc.	/buat/	/buot/	/boot/	/bout/

The intermediate forms have not, of course, replaced the 'original' basilectal and acrolectal forms. Rather, the continuum resulting from dialect contact takes the form of two poles at the extremities consisting of, respectively, opening and closing diphthongs, with intermediate forms in between.

The intermediate forms which are transitional between the opening and closing diphthongs are /ie/ and /uo/ – which are themselves opening diphthongs, but *less* so than /ia/ and /ua/ – and the monophthongs /ee/ and /oo/. The transitions /ie/ > /ee/ > /ei/, and /uo/ > /oo/ > /ou/ are entirely unsurprising and, even allowing for the fact that Cooper does not present us with the detailed phonetics, /ee/ and /oo/ do at first sight seem to represent the shortest route from /ie/ to /ei/, and from /uo/ to /ou/. Notice, however, that an alternative route is also available:

$$*/ie/ > /ii/ > /ei/$$
$$*/uo/ > /uu/ > /uo/$$

There may be a number of reasons why this route was not followed, but doubtless the role of homonymic clash, which we argued in chapter 1 was important in the accommodation process, was of considerable relevance, since /ii/ and /uu/ already occur in the lexical sets of *beat* and *boot*.

It is less easy to account for the transitions /ia/ > /ie/ > /ee/ and /ua/ > /uo/ > /oo/, with the intermediate forms /ie/ and /uo/. These are certainly not unexpected, but the problem is to explain why they occur rather than the alternatives:

$$*/ia/ > /ea/ > /ee/$$
$$*/ua/ > /oa/ > /oo/$$

One possible explanation may lie in the necessity of acquiring, *en route* from basilect to acrolect, the vowels /ie/ and /uo/ anyway in the lexical sets of *fear* and *tour*. Problems of homonymic clash would not occur, assuming that *face* and *fierce* are not distinguished until *face* has acquired /ee/:

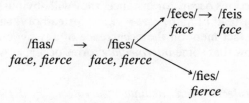

Whatever the explanation, it is encouraging to note that new-dialect or dialect continuum formation, as a macro-level dialect contact phenomenon, and accommodation, at the micro level, do seem susceptible to the same sort of processes and constraints. This, of course, should follow if the former takes place by means of the latter. If new dialects (or, in this case, continua) arise out of contact between dialects, accommodation between individuals involved in the initial contact must have taken place.

We must, however, note at this point that this whole scenario is controversial. Bickerton, for instance, has recently argued (forthcoming) that so-called post-Creole continua have existed for as long as Creoles, at least in the Caribbean area. He also argues that the continua did not result from contact between acrolect and basilect giving rise to mesolect, as we have supposed. Rather, the order of development was acrolect–mesolect–basilect (Creole), with the most basilectal varieties resulting from situations where native (English) speakers were increasingly outnumbered by African slaves, who therefore had only the most limited opportunities for learning the target language. If Bickerton's hypothesis is correct, then at least some post-Creole continua arose not out of dialect contact at all, but directly out of the language contact that, obviously, gives rise to Creoles in the first place.

Focusing along social dialect continua: divergent dialect communities

Our assumption in this chapter has been that the juxtaposition of two distantly related varieties – English and Creole – in St Kitts and Nevis has led to the development, in a diffuse situation, of a diffuse continuum of varieties between these two original dialects. In other situations, however, if the conditions are right, the same sort of two-dialect contact may ultimately give rise to a new relatively focused and discrete variety.

A development of this type is described in the detailed and valuable work of the Swedish sociolinguist Mats Thelander (1979), carried out in Burträsk, northern Sweden (see map 3.3). In his study, Thelander isolated twelve phonological and morphological variables, in the Labovian manner, in the Swedish spoken in Burträsk, and investigated the speech of 56 informants in both formal and informal situations. Burträsk is a *divergent dialect* community, like many other places in Scandinavia (and indeed like most places in northern Britain, but unlike most parts of North America and southern England). This simply means that Burträsk is an area where there is a considerable amount of linguistic distance between the local dialect and the national standard. In divergent dialect communities, it is quite normal to find situational dialect-switching. If this is also the case in Burträsk, it would mean that it is a community rather different from those initially studied by sociolinguists in places like the USA and southern England. In the New York City study by Labov (1966), for instance, speakers clearly do not switch dialects. Rather, they simply decrease or increase the proportions of different variants they employ in different situations. In more recent work in sociolinguistics, however, researchers have turned their attention to areas such as Scotland and Northern Ireland (e.g. Milroy, 1981; Johnston, 1984) where dialect-switching does occur.

In order to investigate whether or not dialect-switching occurs in Burträsk, Thelander distinguishes in his research between *variant-switching* (*variantväxling*) or microvariation, and *variety-switching* or

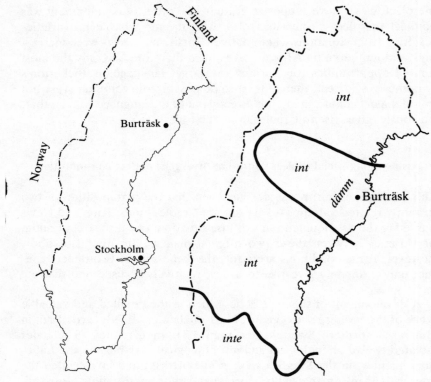

Map 3.3   Location of Burträsk; and geographical limits of *dämm* and *int*
(after Thelander, 1979)

macrovariation. He then comes to grips with the complexity of the
situation by employing quantitative techniques, and distinguishes
between two different types of variant-switching, *integrated* and *isolated*. Switching is labelled 'integrated' if it can be shown that there is
significant covariation of particular variants of different variables. (For
example, integrated variant-switching might be found in an English
speech community if variant [ʔ] of (t) in *bet* co-occurred with variant Ø
of (h) in *hill*, while the other variants [t] and [h] similarly co-occurred.)

Thelander argues that if integrated microvariation does occur in
Burträsk, then this could be a sign that macrovariation or dialect-
switching is taking place. He investigates this possibility by examining
the degree of cohesion between variables by means of a *coefficient of
cohesion*.

Each of Thelander's 12 variables has a standard and a non-standard
variant. Seven of these variables, in the recorded material as a whole,

show a predominance of standard variants (between 51 and 75 per cent). Thelander labels these variables *dialect indicators*, since usage of the non-standard variants of these variables is a particularly strong indication that a speaker is employing non-standard dialect. An example is the variable *dåmm* 'they', which has the standard variant *dåmm* and the dialect variant *dämm*.

The other five variables have fewest standard variants (between 15 and 38 per cent) and are labelled *standard indicators*: usage of the standard variant of these variables is a good indication that the standard is being spoken. An example is *inte* 'not', with the standard variant *inte* and the non-standard variant *int*.

Measurements employing the co-occurrence coefficient mentioned above show that there are indeed tendencies to cohesion in Burträsk. Three major trends are discernible. First, a minority of speakers, in a minority of situations, exhibit co-occurrence of the standard variants of all variables, showing that they are speaking the standard variety. Similarly, some speakers demonstrate co-occurrence of different non-standard variants, showing that they are speaking dialect. Most interestingly, however, a majority of speakers, in a majority of situations, demonstrate a tendency to co-occurrence of the non-dialect variants of dialect indicators with non-standard forms of standard indicators. Thelander argues that the degree of cohesion present between these variants is sufficient to signal the existence of a new *intermediate* variety – intermediate between dialect and standard. He demonstrates by statistical means that this intermediate dialect is a discrete variety with a validity of its own – a dialect, as it were, in its own right.

We imagine, in fact, a chronological development as follows. Contact between the local Burträsk dialect and standard Swedish gave rise over time to the development, as in St Kitts and Nevis, of a continuum between the two (the continuum having more to do with mixtures of different proportions of forms from the two varieties than with the growth of linguistically intermediate forms: see below). Subsequently, *focusing* has taken place at a certain point along this standard–dialect continuum, with a new dialect coalescing around the mixture at a particular level.

Thelander labels this new variety the *regional standard*, referring to the fact that it is spoken over a wider geographical area than that covered by the local Burträsk village dialect, although it does not have such wide usage as the national standard. The relationship between the three varieties involved can be portrayed as in figure 3.3. This shows that, while the standard is characterized by the combination of *dåmm* and *inte* and the local dialect by *dämm* and *int*, the new regional standard combines *int* with *dåmm*.

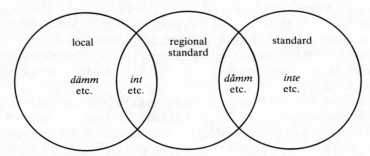

Figure 3.3   Regional standard formation

Of course, if we are trying to achieve a better understanding of dialect contact processes, we would like to be able to explain why the new Burträsk regional standard consists of this particular combination of original dialect and standard forms, and not some other. Thelander argues in fact that the answer lies in the extent of geographical spread of the features concerned. Those non-standard dialect forms which survive in the regional standard are precisely those which are most widespread in northern Swedish dialects (see map 3.3). The major mechanism involved in the formation of the new dialect – and we shall discuss this further below – seems to be the shedding of forms that are marked as being regionally restricted.

As we noted above, the new intermediate dialect has not resulted from the growth of new word-forms that are phonologically intermediate between two original forms, but rather through the combination of original forms into a previously non-occurring mixture. It therefore seems to be the case that new-dialect formation, at least in two-dialect contact situations, can take place through either of two *incomplete accommodation* processes. In the St Kitts-Nevis situation, we see the development, in part, of *phonetically intermediate* forms of the sort that give rise to the process of *approximation* (see p. 61) and the growth of *fudged dialects* (see p. 60), leading to a continuum between two contact dialects. In Burträsk, we see accommodation leading to *alternation* between forms of the sort that gives rise to the process of *transfer* (see p. 60) and the growth of *mixed dialects* (see p. 59). It is very gratifying to see that precisely the same processes that are at work in individual accommodation in face-to-face interaction (see chapter 1), and in the geographical diffusion of linguistic forms (see chapter 2), are also of great importance in new-dialect formation. It gives us confidence, too, that the process of accommodation is central not only to the diffusion of linguistic forms, but also to other dialect contact processes.

Dialect transplantation: new towns

The formation of the new dialect in Burträsk was possible because, in that dialect divergent community, there was sufficient linguistic distance between the two dialects in the original contact situation, leaving room as it were for the formation, as in northern Uruguay, of the new variety. This is also typically the case, we have argued, in situations involving language transplantation of various sorts, and we now return to this type of situation, concentrating first on dialect mixture as this occurs in so-called 'new towns'.

There are many towns in Europe where governments have deliberately created whole new urban areas in an almost virgin landscape, such as Cumbernauld, Scotland, or where small towns have been deliberately expanded into much larger ones, such as Stevenage and Corby, England.

One such new town that has been subjected to close linguistic analysis is Høyanger, Norway. Høyanger is an industrial town in western Norway (see map 2.8) that in 1916, before industrial development, had 120 inhabitants. By 1920 it had 950, and today it has around 3000. The town lies on the border between two western Norwegian dialect areas: the Sogn and the Fjordane dialect zones. Inevitably, however, the small number of original inhabitants who spoke the local, transitional dialect were swamped after 1915 by incomers from elsewhere. Figures from 1920, when the development of the aluminium industry was already under way, show that 28 per cent of the population came from the immediate vicinity of Høyanger and 32 per cent from elsewhere in the county of Sogn og Fjordane. Most of the remaining 40 per cent were from Hordaland (see map 2.8) including Bergen, but there were many also from Telemark, Nordland, and the Oslo area.

According to Omdal (1976, 1977), the current linguistic situation is that the oldest generation in Høyanger – those who for the most part moved into the town from outside – speak dialects that still to a considerable extent reflect the area of the country where they grew up. The second generation – those who were born to the original in-migrants or who came to Høyanger as young children and were brought up there in the 1920s and 1930s – still speak dialects which show to a certain extent the influence of their parents' regional dialects, with considerable variation between speakers. It is only the third generation, often the grandchildren of the original in-migrants, who speak a relatively unified and distinctive Høyanger dialect.

The evidence (see also Ølmheim, 1983) indicates the following scenario, chronologically speaking, for the development of the new dialect.

In the early days of the expansion of Høyanger, the population speaking the indigenous dialect was increasingly outnumbered by speakers of transplanted dialects brought from other parts of Norway. There was therefore enormous variation in the Norwegian spoken in Høyanger. However, it must also have been the case that, through a complex series of accommodation processes – since there were many different dialects to accommodate to – speakers began to reduce differences between their speech, possibly less by acquiring features from other varieties than by reducing or avoiding features in their own varieties that were in some way unusual. Salience and demographic factors would have been vital here, as in diffusion.

The second generation of the new-town inhabitants were influenced, it appears, in the development of their native dialects, not only by their parents' speech but also by the mixture of dialects they heard around them. Which aspects of the mixture made their way into their dialects would depend on their social networks; on the proportions of different dialects present in the mixture; on the degree to which these different dialects did and did not share the same features; and undoubtedly also on the salience and naturalness of particular linguistic features present in the mixture. There would also have been, in this rather diffuse situation, influence from nearby urban dialects, and influence from the standard Norwegian of the schools and the media. (Since 1945, the form of standard Norwegian employed in Høyanger schools has been Nynorsk rather than Bokmål. Nynorsk was, in its development, based to a considerable extent on western Norwegian dialects.)

There was, then, in this generation, a greater degree of similarity between the speech of individual speakers than in the first generation, but still a very large degree of variability between speakers and *within* the speech of individuals. For example, people brought up in Høyanger in this generation might alternate the original western dialect form /æ:g/ 'I' (cf. standard Nynorsk *eg*) with the eastern, and Bokmål, form *jeg* /jei/. Similarly, western *ikkje* 'not' alternated in Høyanger with eastern *ikke*.

In the third generation, however, more complete focusing took place, with a further reduction of variant forms, and with all speakers sharing a more or less common dialect. In this generation, for instance, everyone says /æ:g/ and *ikkje*. Thus, in the space of three generations, a complex dialect mixture situation has been replaced by a new, unified, focused, identifiable dialect. The focusing process may have been aided by the fact that, while workers and managers originally lived in different parts of the town, this is today no longer the case. As a consequence, there is little social dialect differentiation amongst the youngest generation.

We are particularly interested here in the linguistic aspects of focusing, and would like to be able to explain why the modern Høyanger dialect has the particular form it does. Why have some elements in the original mixture survived, and some not? Why has *ikkje* won, and *ikke* lost? Can we account for these developments, supposing they result from accommodation, however complex, in the same way that we accounted for what happens in more straightforward two-dialect contact?

That the new Høyanger dialect has arisen out of dialect mixture is clear from an examination of its linguistic characteristics. This reveals components from many different contributing dialects. The variety remains *basically* a western Norwegian dialect, which is what one would expect given that around half the inhabitants in 1920 were from Sogn og Fjordane. However, there are many elements present in the new dialect which have clearly come from elsewhere. These include, first, forms which are found in Bokmål and in eastern Norwegian dialects:

	original dialect	*Nynorsk*	*Bokmål*	*modern Høyanger*
'to see'	sjao	sjå	se	se
'to say'	seia	seia	si	si
'been'	vori	vore	vært	vært
'each'	kvar	kvar	hver	hver
'someone'	nokon	nokon	noen	noen
'to hear'	håyre	høyre	høre	høre

But there is, secondly, one form that can only have been imported from the dialect of the town of Bergen:

	original dialect	*Nynorsk*	*Bokmål*	*modern Høyanger*
'home'	haim	heim	hjem	hæm

The Bergen form is /hem/.

And there is also one form clearly derived from eastern dialects:

	colloquial eastern	*Nynorsk*	*Bokmål*	*modern Høyanger*
'how'	åssen	korleis	hvordan	åssen

Now, as we have seen, the new dialect crystallized out of a diffuse, amorphous situation in the space of three generations. In the initial mixture there were many different dialects, and even after many years there was still a great deal of variability. Clearly, the process of focusing which led to the emergence of the modern Høyanger dialect out of this variability must necessarily have involved a considerable reduction in the number of linguistic forms available. Of the variants initially available in the mix, most have disappeared leaving, most often, one variant as the sole survivor.

Levelling: Høyanger

As we indicated above, the mechanisms by which this reduction of forms has been achieved are of very considerable interest. One of the major mechanisms we may label *levelling*. Levelling, in this sense, is to be interpreted as implying the reduction or attrition of *marked* variants (see Moag, 1977). In Høyanger, it emerges that *marked* refers, for the most part, to forms that are unusual or in a minority in Norwegian as a whole. That is, it appears that, exactly as in Burträsk, the forms with the widest geographical (and social) usage are the ones that are retained. Examples of the levelling out of marked variants in the formation of the new Høyanger dialect include the following:

(1) Most Norwegian varieties, including the two standard varieties, have a 2 × 9 vowel system of the type:

y:	i:	ʉ:	u:		Y	ɪ	ʉ	ʊ
ø:	e:		o:	œ	ɛ			ɔ
	æ:		ɑ:			æ		a

However, dialects in the area around Høyanger normally differ from this rather radically. First, most Sogn dialects have the long high vowels, elsewhere /y:, i:, ʉ:, and u:/ as diphthongs, e.g. *is* [eis] 'ice'. Secondly, in inner Sogn dialects and, crucially, the original Høyanger dialect, the long vowel /o:/ (orthographic *å*), which most often goes back to an Old Norse long *á*, is realized as diphthongal [ɑo].

Diphthongal realizations of /y:, i:, ʉ:, u:/ are confined to a rather small area of the Norwegian west, while diphthongal realizations of *å* are found only in certain areas of the west (see map 3.4). They are very much minority forms in Norway – geographically restricted and linguistically aberrant in Norwegian terms. It is therefore not remarkable that dialect mixture and new-dialect formation have led to the levelling out – that is, disappearance – of these diphthongal forms in the new Høyanger dialect. Høyanger is now therefore an island of monophthongs in a sea of the typically western Norwegian diphthongs, as a result of the levelling process.

(2) The original, pre-1916 Høyanger dialect had, as neighbouring dialects still do, a voiced palatal affricate /ɟj/ (where, of course, /j/ represents [ʝ], a voiced palatal fricative) in items such as /ryɟjən/ 'the back'. This consonantal articulation is confined to certain areas of western Norway and is unknown in the majority of Norwegian dialects. This consonant, too, has disappeared from the new Høyanger dialect.

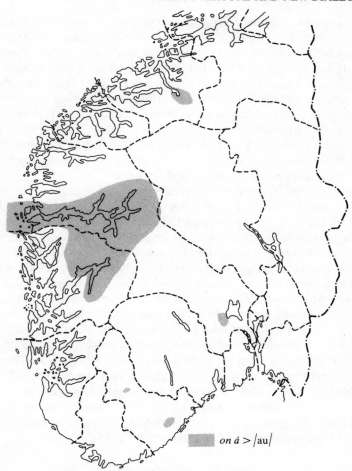

Map 3.4   Diphthongal realizations of *å*, Norway (from K. Chapman, *Icelandic–Norwegian Relationships* (1962), Oslo, Universiteitsforlaget. Reprinted by permission of Norwegian University Press)

Levelling: Fiji

Now by no means all of the variant reduction that we can reconstruct as having occurred during the focusing period in the growth of the Høyanger dialect can be ascribed to levelling. However, before we look at the other major mechanism involved (*simplification*), we turn to another new-dialect formation situation to examine the role played by levelling there, in contrast to Høyanger, in order to assure ourselves that levelling is indeed likely to be of importance in most new-dialect formation contexts.

It is, of course, not only European languages that have been involved in dialect mixture. A number of south Asian languages, for instance, have been transplanted to other areas of the world and become involved in new-dialect formation and other processes there: Tamil in Malaysia and Singapore; Panjabi in Britain; Gujerati in East Africa; and, especially, varieties of Hindi. Hindi is today spoken natively by sizeable populations in many places outside India, including South Africa and Singapore. In particular, however, varieties from the north Indian Indo-Aryan dialect continuum centring on Hindi have since the nineteenth century been involved in mixing and the evolution of new varieties in Fiji, Mauritius, Trinidad, Guyana, and Surinam.

The cover term *Hindustani* has often been used to refer to all those varieties from the north-central Indian dialect continuum bounded by Bengali on the east and Marathi on the west. *Hindi* is the autonomous standard superposed variety which is employed by Hindus, written in the Devanagari script, and has learned loans from Sanskrit. *Urdu* is the autonomous standard superposed variety, very similar to Hindi, which is employed by Moslems, written in the Perso-Arabic script, and has loans from Arabic and Persian. However, the transplanted varieties are derived for the most part not from standard Hindi but from the (mainly Bihari) part of the dialect continuum commonly referred to by the linguistic label *Bhojpuri* (see Shukla, 1981), covering in geographical terms parts of the modern states of Bihar, Uttar Pradesh, and Nepal. Peasants from the Bhojpuri-speaking area of India were, from 1830 to 1920, taken by the British to work as indentured labourers in British colonies and other areas overseas. Currently, people of Indian origin, most of them Bhojpuri speakers, constitute proportions of the populations of these countries as follows (see Holm, 1985):

Trinidad	36 per cent
Surinam	37 per cent
Fiji	50 per cent
Guyana	55 per cent
Mauritius	67 per cent

The linguistic situation in all these areas is of considerable interest, particularly in so far as Bhojpuri/Hindi is concerned. As a result of transplantation, contact with other languages, mixing, and independent developments, new varieties have grown up which differ very strikingly and significantly both from the peasant speech of the nineteenth century and from the modern standard.

In Fiji, people of Indian origin make up half of the population. They are the descendants of indentured labourers who were brought from northern India to work on the sugar plantations during the period 1880–1914. A uniform, mixed dialect of 'Hindustani' has developed which is now known as *Fiji Hindi*, while standard Hindi is taught in schools there.

The Hindi of Fiji has been dealt with by a number of writers, notably Moag (1977) and Miranda (ms.). Their work, indeed, is particularly useful when we come to look for actual *explanations* for the precise form taken by the levelling process. If we are concerned to investigate why some forms are lost and others survive, then Moag suggests that Fiji Hindi differs from Indian varieties of the language through the levelling out of *socially* marked forms, such as honorific pronouns, as well as of regionally marked forms as in Norway. Moag argues that the process of selection, as we saw in the case of Høyanger, while it does indeed favour forms common to a *majority* of the contributing dialects, also favours forms with minimal social and linguistic marking. Very interesting interdialect forms not present in the contributing varieties also occur both as a result of borrowing in one linguistic subsystem from other related subsystems in order to resolve dialect conflicts, and also as a result of systemic pressures. The whole process has been accompanied by the emergence of a single set of uniform norms, through focusing.

The loss of marked minority forms is illustrated in the following data (from Miranda, ms.), comparing modern Fiji Hindi with that of its main contributing Indian dialects:

	standard Hindi	Bhojpuri	Awadi	Fiji Hindi
'what'	kja:	ka:	ka:	ka:
'someone'	koi:	keu:~kauno	koi:~keu:	koi:
'from'	se	se~sẽ	se~te	se
'in'	mẽ	mā:	mẽ	mẽ
'our'	hama:ra:	hama:r	hama:r	hama:r
'one's own'	apna:	a:pan	a:pan	a:pan
'who'	kaun	kaun~ke	kaun~ko	kaun

Clearly, in each case the form which occurs in two or more of the contributing dialects is the one which wins out in the new mixed dialect. However, this cannot be the whole story since, as we have already noted, in some instances intermediate, interdialect forms occur, particularly it seems when there is no form with a clear majority:

	standard Hindi	Bjopuri	Awadi	Fiji Hindi
'who (rel.)'	ɟo	ɟe	ɟo~jaun	ɟon
'with'	sa:th	saŋe	saŋgh	saŋge
'your'	tumha:ra:	tuha:r	tumha:r	tuma:r

In the other cases, minority forms are the ones which remain in the new dialect. In these cases we must therefore seek more narrowly linguistic explanations, in terms of notions such as linguistic markedness. In some cases, for example, it appears to be the *shortest* form which is retained:

	standard Hindi	Bojpuri	Awadi	Fiji Hindi
'this'	jah	i	iu	i
'something'	kuch	kuchu~kichu	kuchu	kuch
'this much'	itna:	etana:	etana:	itna:

In one case, a non-nasal ending survives at the expense of forms with (phonologically marked) nasal vowels:

	standard Hindi	Bojpuri	Awadi	Fiji Hindi
optative first-person plural	-ē:	-ī:	-i:	-i:

In some cases there is no obvious explanation at all:

	standard Hindi	Bojpuri	Awadi	Fiji Hindi
'to'	ko	ke	ka:	ke
'here'	jahā:	ihā:	hijā:	hijā:
'there'	wahā:	uhā:	huwā:	huwā:

In any case, however, we have seen in both Norwegian and Hindi that levelling is clearly an important mechanism in new-dialect formation. In complex dialect-mixture situations, the particular variant from all those available which survives will depend on which one speakers actually accommodate to (or simply acquire, in the case of young children), which in turn will often depend on how *common* it is, and on how *natural* it is. The 'accommodating out' of minority features, as we saw in Høyanger (p. 98), probably occurs already in the first generation of dialect contact. The role of naturalness in the selection of linguistic forms is more likely to be influential, again as we saw in Høyanger, in the second generation, amongst young children.

Simplification: Høyanger

If we return now to the situation in Høyanger, we can note that a very great deal of the variant-reduction process seems to have taken place not through levelling but by means of a process we can call *simplifica-*

tion. Simplification is, of course, a difficult and perhaps dangerous notion. Mühlhäusler has argued (1977) that simplification can be taken to refer to 'an increase in regularity', and that it is a term which should be used *relatively*, with reference to some earlier stage of the variety or varieties in question. There are, according to Mühlhäusler, two main types of simplification. The first type involves an increase in morphophonemic regularity, and would include the loss of inflections and an increase in invariable word forms. Mühlhäusler also points to Ferguson's (1959) similar discussion, where the following are listed as indications of simplification: symmetrical paradigms; fewer obligatory categories marked by morphemes of concord; and simpler morphophonemics.

The second aspect of simplification involves an increase in the 'regular correspondence between content and expression', which is intended to refer to an increase in morphological and lexical transparency: e.g. German *Zahnarzt* 'tooth-doctor' is more transparent than English *dentist*.

Linguistic forms which are candidates for the label of simplification in Høyanger include the following:

(1) Most Norwegian dialects, together with standard Nynorsk, have two different plural endings, unlike Bokmål, which has only one regular ending, namely *-er*. The two endings in Nynorsk are *-er* and *-ar*. The *-ar* ending occurs with most masculine nouns, such as *hest* 'horse', *hestar* 'horses', but a small number of masculines such as *benk* 'bench' take *-er*. Similarly, the majority of feminine nouns take *-er*, such as *vise* 'song', *viser* 'songs', but a number such as *myr* 'bog' take *-ar*. The new Høyanger dialect has neither of these systems. It has not gone over to an undifferentiated, Bokmål-type plural-marker, but it *has* completely regularized the gender differentiation in the plural marking system: *-ar* is employed with all masculines and *-er* with all feminines, except that, as is normal with northern Vestland dialects, the /r/ is absent:

	original dialect	Nynorsk	Bokmål	Modern Høyanger
'horses'	hæsta	hestar	hester	hæsta
'benches'	bænkje	benker	benker	bænka
'songs'	vise	viser	viser	vise
'songs'	myra	myrar	myrer	myre

This represents a clear case of simplification, with irregularities being removed. Though not actually simpler than Bokmål, the new Høyanger system is simpler than standard Nynorsk and the surrounding local dialects. The forms *bænka* and *myre* are clearly *interdialect* forms that have arisen in Høyanger itself, out of interaction between competing dialects, and can perhaps be ascribed to imperfect accommodation by adults. Certainly, however, they also remind us very strongly of what we saw in chapter 1: that there are limits to accommodation even in the case of young children who, if they are not exposed to particular contrasts *ab initio*, may never acquire them at all. It is also, of course, not remarkable that, in a dialect competition situation, forms which are more regular and therefore more learnable actually win out. (Note that this simpler system is increasingly to be found in other Norwegian areas also: L. Maehle, personal communication.)

(2) Many western Norwegian dialects, including the original Høyanger dialect, have morphophonemic alternations between velar and palatal consonants, as in:

tak	/ta:k/	'roof'	/ta:cçə/	'the roof'
rygg	/ryg/	'back'	/ryɟjən/	'the back'

The modern Høyanger dialect no longer has this type of alternation and has instead, as in eastern dialects, *rygg:ryggen* etc. As we saw above, as a result of this development, the consonant /ɟj/ has been lost from Høyanger Norwegian altogether. (On the other hand, the loss of the /k/: /cç/ alternation has not led to the loss of /cç/ since this remains in forms where no alternations occur, such as *ikkje* /ɪcçə/ 'not'.) This, again, represents a clear increase in morphophonemic regularity, or simplification, in the new mixed dialect of Høyanger.

(3) Many of the dialects of western Norway (see Haugen, 1976; Vigeland, 1981) have two forms of the post-posed feminine definite article. So-called 'strong' nouns – those that end in a consonant or stressed vowel – take the suffix -*i*; whereas 'weak' nouns – those that end in an unstressed vowel – take -*a*, thus:

bygd	'village'	*bygdi*	'the village'
jente	'girl'	*jenta*	'the girl'

The modern Høyanger dialect, however, has levelled out this alternation and, like much of the rest of Norway, has -*a* throughout:

bygd	*bygda*
jente	*jenta*

The form *bygda* may be regarded as an interdialect form due to simplification, or as having been acquired from contributing dialects, or, more likely, as both.

(4) In a number of verbs, standard Nynorsk together with most west Norwegian dialects has irregular umlauted forms in the present tense, contrasting with Bokmål, which treats these verbs regularly and which has a consistent -*er* present-tense ending. Modern Høyanger dialect has

simplified this situation and, in spite of the influence of the local standard and of the local dialects, gone over to a Bokmål-type system:

	original dialect	Nynorsk	Bokmål	modern Høyanger
å sova	han søve	han søv	han sover	han sove
'to sleep'	'he sleeps'			
å komme	han kjæmme	han kjem	han kommer	han komme
'to come'	'he comes'			

The forms *han sove, han komme* are interdialect forms. The system they are part of is simpler than that of the original dialect, and the word-forms themselves are *intermediate* between the original dialect and Bokmål. Clearly, the partial accommodation process we have seen at work earlier is, as we have argued before, operative in new-dialect formation, as in other forms of dialect contact development.

(5) Another possible candidate for the label of simplification relates to the system of diphthongs, already discussed under *levelling*. It is of considerable interest to note that, while standard Norwegian and a majority of Norwegian dialects have four indigenous diphthongs, and while the original Høyanger dialect had a system of five diphthongs, the modern Høyanger dialect actually has only three:

original dialect	Nynorsk	Bokmåal	modern Høyanger
/ei/	/ei/	/ei/	
/ai/	/ai/	/ai/	/ai/
/øy/	/øy/	/øy/	
/oy/			/oy/
/æʉ/	/æʉ/	/æʉ/	/æʉ/

The modern Høyanger system results from a merger of original dialect /ei/ and /ai/, giving, for example, general Norwegian /jeit/ 'goat', modern Høyanger /jait/; and from a merger of original /øy/ with /oy/, giving general Norwegian /høy/ 'high', modern Høyanger /hoy/. A similar threefold diphthong system exists in neighbouring Sogn dialects. In the dialect mixture situation, this simpler system, with fewer contrasts, has won out, again probably through incomplete accommodation and, crucially, simplification during child language acquisition. As Labov has pointed out (1972: see below), mergers typically win out over distinctions in contact situations.

We have seen, then, that in Høyanger *levelling* and *simplification*, both due to accommodation processes, are crucial in new-dialect formation in contact situations. We follow Moag (1977) in referring to the combination of levelling and simplification as *koinéization* (see below).

Simplification: Trinidad

We have already examined the role of *levelling* in transplanted varieties of Hindi. We now proceed to examine the role of simplification, established as important in Norwegian, in the same way. One problem, however, that we have with transplanted varieties of Hindi which we have not so far encountered is that of distinguishing between the effects of dialect contact on the one hand, and language contact on the other.

In all cases, new dialects of Hindi that have resulted from transplantation and mixing are also in contact with other languages: Fijian, Mauritian French Creole, Trinidadian English, Sranan (in Surinam), and so on. In Fiji, moreover, Hindi is widely used by non-native speakers as a lingua franca in interethnic communication. As a result of this language contact, therefore, the study of *simplification* in these new varieties of Hindi is a little more complex than it typically is in new-town contexts. The fact is that, in the case of colonial Hindi, simplification has been rather more extensive than in many other contact situations, both as a result of pidginization due to lingua franca usage, and as a result of language death due to partial language shift. Language death, of course, is well known to lead to certain sorts of simplification, though not necessarily of exactly the same sort that one would expect to encounter in pidginization or dialect contact (see Dorian, 1973; Trudgill, 1983).

In Trinidad, for example, it is particularly difficult to distinguish between the consequences of koinéization and those of language death. The official language of Trinidad is English, but the most widely spoken language is Trinidadian English Creole, and the vast majority of the Hindi speakers, who constitute about one-third of the population, are bilingual in Hindi and the Creole. Indeed, many of the younger generation of 'Hindi speakers' are actually more fluent in English and/or Creole than in Hindi.

Interference from the Creole in modern Trinidadian Hindi is apparent (see Holm, 1985) in the acquisition by the latter of the perfective aspect marker *done* from the former:

> u da:n gail ɟel
> 'he done went gaol' = he has already gone to jail

There is also considerable lexical borrowing from English.

As far as simplification is concerned, quite radical changes can be noted. For example, Trinidad Hindi has lost gender, number, and case agreement in the noun phrase:

/čoṭa: laṛka:/
'little   boy'
masc.sing.   masc.sing.

/čoṭa: čori/
'little   girl'
masc.sing.   fem.sing.

Similarly, the number of forms in verb paradigms has been greatly reduced (see Mohan, 1978; Bhatia, 1982). The future-tense paradigm of the verb 'to come', for instance, has three forms rather than the original eighteen: honorific inflections have been lost in the second and third persons; feminine inflectional forms have been lost; and there is no longer any singular–plural distinction:

		singular	plural
'will come'	1	a:ib	a:ib
	2	aibe	aibe
	3	a:i:	a:i:

Many irregular Hindi verbs have also become regular in Trinidad.

How much of this simplification is due to language death and language contact and how much to dialect contact is difficult to determine, but obviously the *extent* of the simplification reported for Trinidad Hindi suggests very strongly that, while dialect mixture has been of some considerable importance, it is not the whole story.

Koinéization

We suspect, in any case, a key role for koinéization in new-dialect formation. In dialect contact and dialect mixture situations there may be an enormous amount of linguistic variability in the early stages. However, as time passes, focusing takes place by means of a *reduction* of the forms available. This reduction takes place through the process of koinéization, which consists of the *levelling* out of minority and otherwise marked speech forms, and of *simplification*, which involves, crucially, a reduction in irregularities. (The degree of simplification, and possibly its nature, may be influenced by lingua franca usage (pidginization) and by language death in situations which involve language contact as well as dialect contact.) The result of the focusing associated with koinéization is a historically mixed but synchronically stable dialect which contains elements from the different dialects that went into the mixture, as well as interdialect forms that were present in none.

Variability in mixed dialects: Mauritius

We have seen that the process of new-dialect formation operates through a reduction in variability. However, an important fact about dialects that have recently coalesced out of dialect mixtures is that, even after focusing has taken place, many of them continue to retain, at least for some generations, a relatively high level of variability. Having discussed in the previous section the mechanisms involved in the reduction of available forms, we shall therefore in this section attend to this variability, concentrating on those variant forms which actually still remain in the new dialect, and on the relationships they establish with each other.

We can begin by continuing our examination of transplanted varieties of Hindi. Domingue (1980, 1981) has provided an extremely useful account of the Bhojpuri spoken in modern Mauritius. Mauritius has a population of around one million, of whom 28 per cent are of African origin and native speakers of Mauritian French Creole, which is also the island's informal lingua franca. (Both French and English are official languages.) About 5 per cent of the population are of French or Chinese origin, while 67 per cent or so are of Indian origin. Of these, approximately 83 per cent (i.e. about 555,000 people) are native speakers of Hindi/Bhojpuri.

Bhojpuri in India is classified into four main dialects: eastern, central, western and Nagpurian. The central dialects form the basis of standard Bhojpuri, and have also apparently contributed most to the formation of Mauritian Bhojpuri. Domingue shows that some of the differences between Mauritian and Indian Bhojpuri, as in Trinidad, cannot be ascribed to the results of dialect mixture, but are rather the result of *language* contact, i.e. the influence from French Creole. Features of Mauritian Bhojpuri which seem to have arisen in this way include:

(1) The weakening of subject/object/verb word order in the direction of subject/verb/object;
(2) The loss of the reflexive possessive adjective;
(3) The merger in function of the two copulas *bä* and *ha*.

Of the features of Mauritian Bhojpuri which distinguish it from that of India and which clearly *are* the result of dialect mixture, we can see, as we saw in Fiji, Trinidad, and Høyanger, the effects of both *levelling* and *simplification*. Mauritian Bhojpuri is very uniform indeed, with no regional variation of any significance at all. Clearly, then, differences between eastern, central, western and Nagpurian dialects have been levelled out. Mauritian Bhojpuri, however, is obviously of mixed origin, for while it contains predominantly central dialect features, there are a number of forms from the other dialects, e.g.:

	central	Nagpurian	western	Mauritian
1 possessive	hamār	hamar		hamar
2 possessive	tohār	tōhar		tōhar
3 past	-asa	-ak		-ak
	ãkhi		ãkh	ãkh
	pãkhi		pãkh	pãkh

The different regional options present in the original mixture have been levelled down to one.

As far as simplification is concerned, Domingue provides us with the following examples, amongst others:

(1) In Indian Bhojpuri, there is an instrumental case marker *-ē*. There is also an alternative periphrastic construction using *sē*: thus *būkhē* or *bukh sē* 'out of hunger'. In Mauritius, only the periphrastic construction occurs, the case ending having been lost.

(2) In the Indian Bhojpuri dialects, adjectives optionally agree with animate nouns for gender. In Mauritian Bhojpuri, this agreement rule is no longer a possibility.

(3) In Indian Bhojpuri, verbs have different endings for masculine and feminine subjects. In Mauritius, the feminine endings have been lost except in the past-tense second-person singular.

Koinéization has therefore clearly been at work. However, most interesting for our purposes in this section is the observation that in Mauritian Bhojpuri there are some features for which different variants in the original mixture have *not* been reduced to one. In Mauritius, as we have seen, there is no regional variation. However, in some cases regional variants from the different continental dialects have been retained *without* being levelled out. What has happened, in fact, is that they have been retained in the new, focused dialect as *stylistic variants*. Thus:

	India eastern	India central	western	Mauritius high	Mauritius low
'big'	/bara:/	/baɽa:/		/baɽa:/	/bara:/
'temple'		/mandir/	/mandil/	/mandil/	/mandir/
'road'		/ra:hta/	/ra:sta/	/ra:sta/	/ra:hta/

(There are in fact a number of alternations of this type involving western dialect word-final /l/ with central dialect /r/; and western dialect /s/ in medial clusters with central dialect /h/.)

The new dialect has thus retained some of the regional variants present in the early mixture, but these have been *reallocated* to a stylistic function. This suggests a general principle: forms that are not removed during koinéization, as part of the focusing associated with new-dialect formation, will tend to be reassigned according to certain patterns. One of these patterns is that retained variants may acquire different degrees of formality and be reallocated the function of stylistic variants. We shall now proceed to investigations of other varieties in an attempt to see if further patterns of variant reallocation can be adduced.

Reallocation: Norwich

We look first at the case of linguistic urbanization: the growth not of new-town dialects but of urban dialects through the mixing of (usually) closely related rural dialects from different parts of an expanding city's hinterland. (For a Norwegian study, see Jenstad, 1983.) One such urban dialect in Britain is that of Norwich, as investigated in Trudgill (1974). One thing that became very clear in this study was that in-migration from adjoining rural areas can be of some linguistic consequence, particularly when allied to partial accommodation on the part of adults. All of the informants in the Norwich study had lived all or most of their lives in the city. Some, however, were of rural origin. These speakers tended to differ linguistically from the urban-born at a number of points, although this was usually clear only from quantitative analyses. Table 3.3, for example, shows percentage scores for *h*-dropping for rural-born in-migrants versus the total Norwich sample by style and social class. In each case, the rural-born speakers' indices are lower, i.e. they pronounce more /h/s than the sample as a whole. Clearly, in-migration in very recent times has had an effect on modern Norwich English, albeit of an entirely quantitative nature. It is therefore quite possible that we will be able to explain certain other aspects of the variability present in modern Norwich English in terms of patterns of in-migration and dialect mixture at earlier periods.

One case in point involves three vowels which are distinguished in Norwich English but not in most other varieties (see Wells, 1982). The vowels are:

/ʉ:/ [əʉ] as in *rude*
/u:/ [ʊu] as in *go*
/ʌu/ [ɐu] as in *know*

Table 3.3   Percentage /h/-dropping in Norwich

Class	Word list style		Reading passage style		Formal speech		Casual speech	
	Rural	Total	Rural	Total	Rural	Total	Rural	Total
Lower middle	0	0	0	5	2	4	12	14
Upper working	0	1	0	7	7	24	12	40
Middle working	0	4	4	12	23	43	50	59
Lower working	0	5	8	13	0	41	0	61

Source: Trudgill, 1974.

The relationship between these vowels, as well as /ʊ/ and /jʉː/, as we saw in chapter 1, is a complex one, with lexical sets as follows:

/jʉː/ or /ʉː/	*suit, tune, few, cue* etc.
/ʉː/ only	*do, who, lose, rude*
/ʉː/ or /uː/	*boot, food, fool, mood*
/uː/ only	*go, goal, pool, group*
/uː/ or /ʊ/	*stone, home, coat, road*
/ʊ/ only	*put, pull, foot, roof*
/ʉː/, /uː/ or /ʊ/	*room, broom, proof*
/ʌu/ only	*know, low, old, soul*

Variability may be both intra-individual and, more often, inter-individual.

Of course, Norwich English was never entirely uniform: no dialect ever is. But it is possible that an increase in variability occurred as a result of in-migration over the past several generations, and that, therefore, we can account for the variability involving /ʉː/, /uː/, and /ʊ/ in terms of dialect mixture. We can perhaps begin to do this by attempting, as it were, to pull apart the strands that went into making up the mixture in the first place – and hence the variability – in the following way:

(1) The lexical sets containing /ʊ/ only (*put* etc.) and /ʌu/ only (*know* etc.) are unproblematical. (We saw in chapter 1 that Norwich English distinguishes /ʌu/ in *knows* from /uː/ in *nose* as a result of failing to experience the Early Modern English merger of Middle English ǭ and ou.)

(2) The set containing /jʉː/ or /ʉː/ (*suit* etc.) is the result of dialect mixture of a sort: the alternation is between local forms without /j/, current over much of eastern England (see Wells, 1982 on *yod-dropping*; and Chambers and Trudgill, 1980), and RP-type prestige forms with /j/.

We are now left therefore requiring explanations for the following five lexical sets:

/ʉː/	/uː/	/ʊ/
lose		
boot	boot	
	go	
	stone	stone
room	room	room

(3) Items derived from Middle English ǭ such as *go* and *stone* are all capable of having /uː/ in Norwich. Most, however, also appear to be, or to have been, subject to shortening to /ʊ/, with the consequence that, for example, *road* and *good* rhyme. This shortening is of course not possible in the case of words such as *go* since */gʊ/ etc. is phonotactically impossible in English. The following items are attested with /ʊ/ in East Anglian English (Kökeritz, 1932):

> boast, boat, bone, choke, cloak, clover, coach, coast, coat, don't, folk, goat, hole, home, hope, load, loaf, moat, most, oak, oath, oats, over, poach, pole, post, road, rope, smoke, stone, toad, whole, wholly

in addition (Lowman's records from 1938: see Viereck, 1980):

> comb, froze, ghosts, hotel, woke, won't, wrote, yolk

in addition (Survey of English Dialects: Orton et al., 1962–71):

> both, broke, spoke, throat

in addition (Trudgill, 1974):

> aerodrome, alone, bloke, drove, notice, only, photo, suppose

It seems very likely indeed that shortening was possible in all preconsonantal environments. Alternation between /uː/ and /ʊ/ in the modern dialect is clearly *partly* the result of dialect mixture, i.e. the influence of non-local varieties ousting /ʊ/ in favour of /uː/. W. Nelson Francis writes (ms.) of the oldest Survey of English Dialects informant in Pulham in the 1950s: 'Evidence of shortened lax forms, apparently much more prevalent in the dialect 50–75 years ago, was rather plentiful . . . thus [ɹʊd, stʊn, kʊm, spʊk, tɹʊt] [= *road, stone, comb, spoke, throat*]. The prevalence of /uː/ in the speech of younger persons seems to be the result of standard English influence.' Whether or not this alternation was *entirely* brought about in this way, or whether /ʊ/ has always been simply a stylistic variant, is not clear.

(4) We are left, finally, with relexes of ME ǭ:

/ʉ:/	/u:/	/ʊ/
lose		
boot	boot	
room	room	room

Norwich English consistently has *blood* etc. with /ʌ/ and *good* etc. with /ʊ/ as in RP. It is equally consistent, however, in having /ʊ/ in *roof* and *hoof*. Map 3.5, after the SED, shows that the entire rural hinterland of Norwich has /ʊ/ in *roof* and *hoof*. The consistency in Norwich is therefore not surprising. Similarly, map 3.6 shows the rural hinterland with /ʉ:/ in *lose*, again the consistent Norwich pronunciation.

However, if rural consistency produces consistency in the urban dialect, the reverse is also true. It emerges that for a number of features, Norwich lies at or near isoglosses dividing one rural dialect area from another. As far as ME ǭ is concerned, there are a number of items where /u:/ occurs in the west of Norfolk, /ʉ:/ to the north of Norwich, and /ʊ/ to the south. It is therefore not too surprising that all three of these vowels are found in the urban dialect as competing variants. In-migration has indeed led to variability. Maps 3.7 to 3.13 show that this is so in some detail, and reproduce material from the SED involving items having ME ǭ. Each word seems to demonstrate a rather different pattern, but the following points can be noted:

Map 3.5 *roof, hoof* in East Anglia (after Survey of English Dialects, Orton et al., 1962–71: abbreviated SED in captions to maps 3.6–3.13)

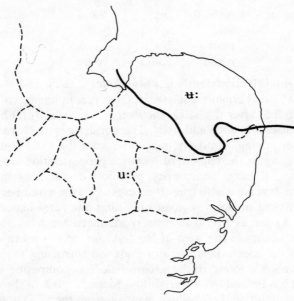

Map 3.6 *lose* in East Anglia (after SED)

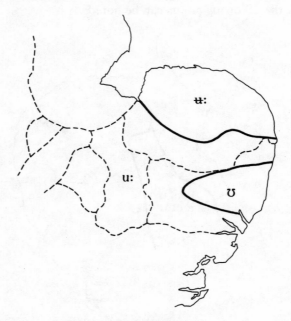

Map 3.7 *afternoon* in East Anglia (after SED)

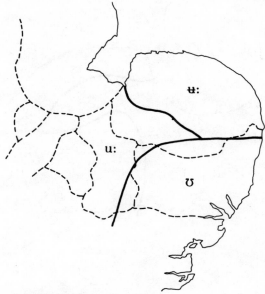

Map 3.8   *root* in East Anglia (after SED)

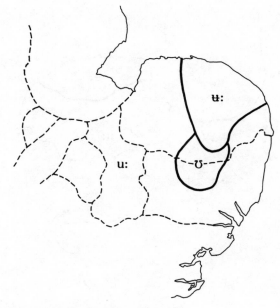

Map 3.9   *goose* in East Anglia (after SED)

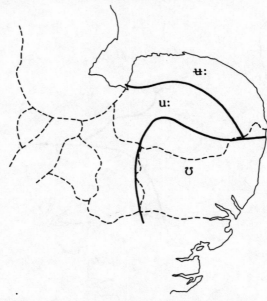

Map 3.10   *whooping* in East Anglia (after SED)

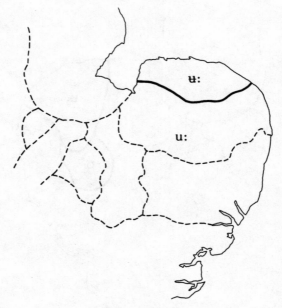

Map 3.11   *school* in East Anglia (after SED)

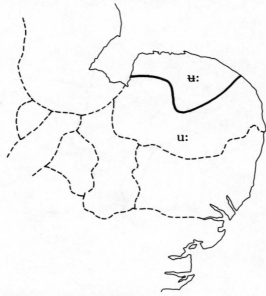

Map 3.12 *stool* in East Anglia (after SED)

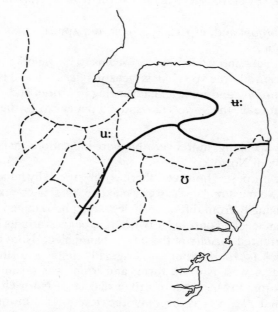

Map 3.13 *broom* in East Anglia (after SED)

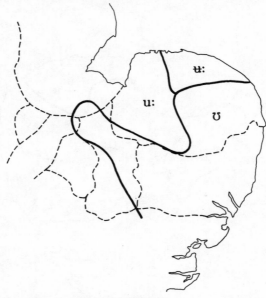

Map 3.14   *room* in East Anglia (after SED)

(1) The vowel /ʉ:/ survives very strongly in Norfolk in *afternoon* and *root*.
(2) In *broom* and, especially, *room*, /ʉ:/ appears to be giving ground to /ʊ/.
(3) In *goose* and *whooping*, /ʉ:/ seems to be yielding to /u:/.
(4) In Suffolk, the vowel /ʊ/ is weak in *afternoon* and *goose*, strong in *whooping* and *root*, and advancing in *broom* and *room*.
(5) Before /l/, the vowels /ʉ:/ and /u:/ appear to be the only possibilities.

Generally speaking, moreover, there are indications that /ʉ:/ is receding into northern Norfolk.

For our purposes, however, there is one especially important observation that we must make. As we saw above, in dialect mixture situations forms originally from different dialects may be retained as alternatives rather than levelled out. In Norwich, it appears, variants if retained may be redistributed *socially* in the new urban dialect. Note that, as is clear from map 3.14, *room* /rʉ:m/ was originally simply a north Norfolk form; /ru:m/ was a west Norfolk form; and /rʊm/ was a south Norfolk and Suffolk form. In the modern urban dialect of Norwich, however, the fact is that /rʉ:m/ has become the low-status, lower-working-class variant, while /ru:m/ has high status and /rʊm/ is of intermediate, lower-middle/upper-working-class status. In addition, that is, to being reallocated a stylistic function, as in Mauritius, non-levelled variants involved in new-dialect formation may be reallocated a *social-class* role in the resulting dialect. In Mauritius, individual speakers select one or the other of the available variants according to stylistic content. In the case of Norwich dialect *room* etc., on the other hand, individual speakers most often use only one pronunciation. Which one they normally use generally correlates very closely with their social-class background.

Reallocation: Belfast

We now examine yet another example of variant reallocation, and once again from English. J. Milroy (1978) writes of the city of Belfast, Northern Ireland, that it is 'a young city, standing at the intersection of two widely divergent dialect areas' (Ulster Scots and mid-Ulster English). This, of course, makes it doubly interesting for the investigation of new-dialect formation. The youth of the dialect – rural migration in large numbers into Belfast continued into the 1920s – means that it may still be possible to see some of the dialect mixture processes at work. And the sharp dialect boundary (see map 3.15) means that it should be simpler than in the case of towns with relatively homogeneous hinterlands to separate out the different components of the original mixture. (The Ulster-Scots-speaking areas of Ireland are those in which the original Irish-speaking population was replaced by Lowland Scots. The mid-Ulster dialect is itself in origin a mixed variety, with Scots dialects and western English English varieties having gone into its formation.)

We can observe, first, that Belfast English demonstrates some of the features we have come in this book to associate with koinéization. For example, as a result of *simplification*, a number of phonemic distinctions present in the rural hinterland have been lost in the new, mixed urban dialect. Labov (1972, p. 300) has suggested, in discussing American English, that this may be a universal process:

> This rapid language mixing seems to follow a kind of classic structural reductionism, and it would not be difficult to argue that it is a sub-type of the same process that produces contact languages. . . . One of the universal constraints on change seems to be operating here – that in contact situations, mergers expand at the expense of distinctions.

(Recall also the merger of /s/ and /z/ in Fronteiriço, p. 85.)

We saw in chapter 1 that children from out-of-town families in Norwich fail to acquire the vocalic *moan:mown* distinction. The work of

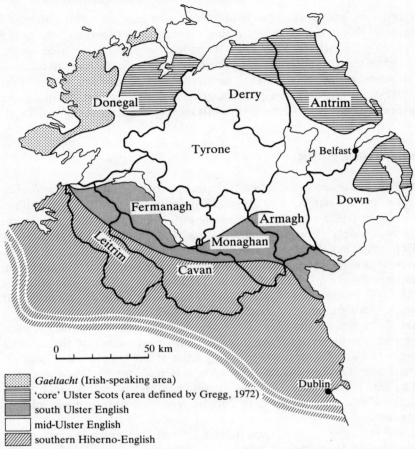

Map 3.15 Approximate boundaries of northern Hiberno-English dialects (from Harris, 1984a)

J. Milroy and L. Milroy (see 1978) in Belfast shows the same sort of phenomenon on a much wider scale, but occurring, presumably, for the same reasons. For example, the vowels /ɪ/, /eɪ/ and /ʌ/, which remain distinct before /r/ in Scots and many parts of Northern Ireland, are merged before /r/ in Belfast, so that *fir*, *fair* and *fur* are now all homophonous. Similarly, the distinction between /w/ and /ʍ/, as in *witch* and *which*, has been lost, in spite of the fact that nearly all other Irish and Scottish varieties retain it. And the vowels of *sort* and *port*, *hoarse* and *horse*, have also been merged.

Moreover, as in Norwich and Mauritius, in those cases where levelling has not taken place, variants have undergone reallocation as social class and/or stylistic indicators. For instance, Belfast English, like Scottish varieties generally, does not distinguish the vowels of *food* and *good*, both sets having the vowel /u/ (see p. 81). However, Belfast English is also characterized by an alternation, in a large but restricted lexical set, between /u/ and /ʌ/ (otherwise found in *up*, *but*, *mud* etc.). The lexical set includes items such as *pull*, *put*, *push*, *full*, *butcher*, *took*, *stood*, *would*. Thus *pull* can be pronounced /pul/, rhyming with *fool*, or /pʌl/, rhyming with *dull*. This alternation forms an interesting and complex sociolinguistic variable in Belfast, with, for example, women employing the /ʌ/ variants on average less frequently than men.

Maclaran (1976, p. 57) writes that this particular aspect of variability in Belfast English has been 'reinforced by regional dialect mix'. Indeed, it can be argued that the phenomenon is entirely *due* to dialect mixture, including standard forms of English as one element in the mixture. The fact is that /ʌ/ in the set of *pull*, *put* is typical of a number of Scots dialects, including Ulster Scots. Mid-Ulster dialects, on the other hand, not only do not have /ʌ/ in this set; many of them (like North of England varieties) do not have /ʌ/ at all, employing /u/ instead (see Henry, 1957); thus:

	RP	north England	mid-Ulster	Ulster Scots	Belfast
but	ʌ	ʊ	u	ʌ	ʌ
put	ʊ	ʊ	u	ʌ	ʌ~u
good	ʊ	ʊ	u	u	u
boot	u:	u:	u	ɪ	u

The Ulster Scots /ʌ/ variants in *put* etc. are now typical of informal styles in Belfast, and of lower-social-class speakers, while the standard /u/ variants in that lexical set are now the more formal, higher-status forms. It seems probable in this case, however, that the alternation, due to reallocation, may disappear in a few decades. Belfast English seems not yet to have completed the focusing process; and the reduction of alternatives that normally accompanies this seems likely eventually to remove the /ʌ/ variant entirely from this set. The number of RP /ʊ/ words in which Belfast /ʌ/ may occur is already a good deal smaller than it was in the nineteenth century (see L. Milroy, 1980).

In addition to the retention of variants as stylistic and social-class indicators, however, Belfast also shows two other forms of reallocation that we have not come across before. The first involves the redistribution of regional dialect differences as *areal variants* within the town itself. The three working-class areas of Belfast investigated by the Milroys were: Ballymacarett, a Protestant area in east Belfast; the Hammer, a Protestant area in the west; and the Clonard, a Catholic area in the west. According to L. Milroy (1980, p. 78), east Belfast has been settled longer than west Belfast, and everywhere Catholics are more likely to be recent arrivals from the rural hinterland than Protestants: 'Every Clonard informant was conscious of having a rural family background. . . . Hammer informants usually had a much vaguer notion that their grandparents were "from the country". . . . In contrast, no Ballymacarett informant had any memory of a rural background at all.' It is nevertheless fairly clear that Ballymacarett was settled originally mostly from northern County Down; the Hammer from Antrim and Armagh; and Clonard from mid-Ulster, west of Armagh. Down and Antrim are in the Ulster Scots rural dialect area, while the other areas are in the mid-Ulster dialect area.

In view of the well-known sharp ethnic division of the Belfast population into Protestants and Catholics, it is perhaps surprising that linguistic differences between the two groups are not especially great. Milroy demonstrates, in fact, that what differences there are are mostly a matter of tendencies and probabilities, but it is apparent that the region of origin of an area's population is still of some importance. For example, the occurrence of [j] before front vowels after velar stops (once widespread in English and still common in the Caribbean) survives in Northern Ireland and is well known as a rural stereotype. In Belfast, pronunciations such as *cap* [cjap], *began* [bəɟjan], *car* [cjaɹ] are rare in modern speech but, in so far as they do occur, are more prevalent in the west than the east, and more common in Clonard than Hammer.

However, it is of considerable interest to notice that the relationship between rural region and city area may not necessarily be a very straightforward one. As we saw above, the vowel /ʌ/ in the lexical set of *pull, put* is Ulster Scots in origin. We would therefore expect it to be most common in Ballymacarett, of the three areas studied. We also saw that /ʌ/ is totally absent from mid-Ulster English. We would therefore expect /ʌ/ in *pull* etc. to be absent from or rare in the Clonard. In fact, the actual situation is the complete reverse of this: low-prestige /pʌl/, /pʌt/ etc. is *most* prevalent in the speech of Clonard informants. Maclaran (1976) writes of this phenomenon that, as mid-Ulster English has no /ʌ/, the first immigrants to the Clonard presumably had no /ʌ/ either. The areas based in the older Ulster-Scots dialect, such as the Hammer and particularly Ballymacarett, would, on the other hand, have had /ʌ/ as in southern England, but in the wider lexical set including *pull, put, stood* etc. She writes, further, that 'since the [ʌ] variant would have been seen as characteristic of the longer-established group, it would probably have acquired prestige for latest arrivals, even though by this stage it was stigmatized by the middle classes.' We can therefore argue that Clonard informants today have a higher usage of /ʌ/ because: (a) they are more isolated from newer prestige norms (based on RP rather than Ulster Scots); and/or (b) they are more conservative than other groups; and/or (c) because, at the time of their forebears' arrival in Belfast, they engaged in the production of *interdialect* forms by means of hyperadaptation. That is, they employed the /ʌ/ forms more than the model (Protestant group) – a form of statistical *Labov-hypercorrection* rather than classic hypercorrection (see Labov, 1966; Wells, 1982). It is even possible that, through hypercorrection in its more usual sense, they extended the vowel /ʌ/ to lexical items where it did not belong, i.e. where it did not occur in Scots or Ulster Scots. In any case, dialect contact seems to have played an important though complex role.

The second form of reallocation that appears in the dialect of Belfast, as a result of urbanization, is one that will turn out to be of some importance in the analysis of English colonial dialects (see chapter 4). J. Milroy (1982) discusses the vowel /a/ in Belfast English – the vowel of the lexical set of *cat, bad, path, calm* etc. – and notes a very great deal of variability indeed in its realization in working-class speech. Variants, in fact, range from [ɛ] through [a] to [ɔ]. Tables 3.4 and 3.5, moreover, show that the entire range can occur in the speech of individuals.

Table 3.4   Realizations of /a/ for a working-class Belfast speaker, conversational style

[ɛ]	[æ]	[a]	[ɑ]	[ɔ]
bang (5)	Bangor	Castlereagh (2)	bad	past
crack (2)	jacket	barracks	Strathearn	plaster
Kojak	back	that (3)	have	palace
avenue	cracking	snap	wrap	hand
		cracking	happen	Belfast (2)
		Albert	Belfast	stand-by
		avenue	Catholic (2)	handsome
		baton (2)	Castlereagh	can
		camera	happy	strand
		Shankill (2)	handsome	
			candid	

Source: after J. Milroy, 1982.

Milroy argues that this range of variability may be characteristic of vernacular varieties generally, while standard varieties, on the other hand, tend to reduce phonological variability. He supports his case by citing the lack of variation in Belfast amongst middle-class speakers, illustrated here as table 3.6. The contrast is clearly quite dramatic. Milroy strengthens his case by *range scores* measuring how many variants of /a/ an informant uses: the working-class speaker has a range of 5

Table 3.5   Realizations of /a/ for a working-class Belfast speaker, word list style

	[ɛ]	[æ]	[a]	[ä]	[ɑ]	[ɔ]
bag	+					
back		+				
cap			+			
map				+		
passage				+		
cab						+
grass						+
bad						+
man						+
castle			+			
dabble			+			
passing						+

Source: after J. Milroy, 1982.

Table 3.6   Realizations of /a/ for a middle-class Belfast speaker, word list style

	[ɛ]	[æ]	[a]	[ä]	[ɑ]	[ɔ]
bag			+			
back			+			
cap			+			
map			+			
passage			+			
cab			+			
grass			+			
bad			+			
man			+			
castle			+			
dabble			+			
passing			+			

Source: after J. Milroy, 1982.

(in addition, that is, to [a]), while the middle-class speaker has a range score of 0. Taking Milroy's 60 informants as a whole, we find the following average scores:

class	*average range*	*range of 1 or less*	*range of 3 or more*
Lower	2.83	4%	67%
Upper	1.97	31%	23%

I would actually prefer to argue that the very wide range of allophones of /a/ in working-class Belfast English – found also in the case of some other vowels – is typical not so much of vernacular varieties as of *mixed varieties*. My suggestion in fact is that different phonological variants present in a dialect mixture situation, and not levelled out during focusing, may be retained as *allophonic variants*. It is clear from Milroy's tables that the reallocation process in this relatively young dialect is not yet entirely complete: there is only, for example, a *tendency* for [ɛ] to occur before velar consonants and [ɔ] before nasals. But the development of regular allophones in complementary distribution may not be far off. We shall produce further evidence for this development in chapter 4.

Reallocation and accommodation

Reallocation, of course, poses certain problems concerning the role of accommodation in dialect contact situations: why is it, for instance, that certain variants are *not* levelled out; and why are the variants that remain reallocated as they are, rather than in some other way? We can only make a beginning to answering these two questions, but we can note that variant retention implies *lack of accommodation*. Our observations on accommodation in chapter 1 may therefore point to a partial solution to the first question. There we saw that forms that are not accommodated to are either of low salience or of very high salience: that is, *extra-strong salience* may inhibit accommodation. The latter factor appears the more likely to provide an explanation for why the lexical set of *room* behaves as it does in Norwich dialect, as the alternation between /u:/, /ʉ:/ and /ʊ/ in the set of *room* is, obviously, an alternation between surface phonemes. (The same is true of /u/ and /ʌ/ in Belfast.) It is at least possible, therefore, that initially speakers of the three different Norfolk dialects had the same difficulty accommodating to each other in respect of the pronunciation of *room* as English people have accommodating to the American pronunciation of *dance*. As a result, none of the three variants present in the mixture in Norwich gave way to any of the others.

This will not, however, work as an explanation where forms remain as stylistic or allophonic variants, since individual speakers in these cases use more than one variant. We deal with allophonic variants in more detail in chapter 4. As far as stylistic variants are concerned, we can say that full (as opposed to pidgin) language varieties appear to *need* stylistic variation (see Labov, ms.), and dialect mixture provides an ideal source for variation of this type to be acquired.

As far as the second question is concerned, we can do no better than come up with an *ad hoc* explanation in each case. The 'high' variants in Mauritian Bhojpuri, for instance, appear to be those most like standard Hindi. And, in the case of Norwich vowels, the fact that RP normally has /u:/ in *room* explains why this is the higher-social-class variant of the three. However, why /ʊ/ and /ʉ:/ are socially ordered as they are is not clear, unless it is because some RP speakers do employ /ʊ/.

Conclusion

We can now summarize our findings as follows. In a dialect mixture situation, large numbers of variants will abound, and, through the process of *accommodation* in face-to-face interaction, *interdialect* phenomena will begin to occur. As time passes and *focusing* begins to take place, particularly as the new town, colony, or whatever begins to acquire an independent identity, the variants present in the mixture begin to be subject to *reduction*. Again this presumably occurs via accommodation, especially of salient forms. This does not take place in a haphazard manner, however. In determining who accommodates to whom, and which forms are therefore lost, demographic factors involving proportions of different dialect speakers present will clearly be vital. More importantly, though, more purely linguistic forces are also at work. The reduction of variants that accompanies focusing, in the course of *new-dialect formation*, takes place via the process of *koinéization*. This comprises the process of *levelling*, which involves the loss of marked and/or minority variants; and the process of *simplification*, by means of which even minority forms may be the ones to survive if they are linguistically simpler, in the technical sense, and through which even forms and distinctions present in all the contributory dialects may be lost. Even after koinéization, however, some variants left over from the original mixture may survive. Where this occurs, *reallocation* may occur, such that variants originally from different regional dialects may in the new dialect become *social-class dialect variants, stylistic variants, areal variants*, or, in the case of phonology, *allophonic variants*.

4

Koinéization in Colonial English

As we have seen, dialect mixture and new-dialect formation are well known to occur in transplanted language situations. In this chapter we examine koinéization in colonial varieties of English, using *colonial* as a technical term covering in principle all types of English other than those spoken in England and the lowlands of Scotland – the part of the world to which English was almost entirely confined until the seventeenth century, which is to say for most of its history. Those varieties of English that are spoken elsewhere in the world – the colonial varieties – have resulted from movements of people outwards from Britain, from the seventeenth century onwards, often involving dialect mixture; the influence of other languages with which English has come into contact; and independent developments that have occurred subsequently in different parts of the world, some of them in response to new environments and new uses. These colonial varieties include the forms of English spoken in the Highlands of Scotland, in Wales, in the English county of Cornwall (which has been entirely English speaking only since the seventeenth or eighteenth centuries), and in Ireland, the Isle of Man, Canada, the United States of America, Central America, South America, the Caribbean, the Bahamas, Bermuda, St Helena, Tristan da Cunha, the Falkland Islands, Liberia, East Africa, South Africa, Zimbabwe, Australia, and New Zealand, as well as in many other areas of the world where second-language and/or pidginized and creolized forms of English are to be found.

Our examination of colonial varieties of English will attempt to distinguish between the effects of dialect contact, language contact, and independent developments, but, as we shall see, this is not always easy or even possible.

It will be recalled that the term 'koinéization' covers the processes of mixing, levelling, and simplification. We therefore begin our examination of koinéization in colonial English by examining the process of dialect *mixing*. First, though, we must note that we cannot always expect to be sure of finding that mixing has occurred in colonial situations. Obviously, if the transplantation involves only one dialect, then there will be no dialect contact in the new location, and therefore no dialect mixture.

Falkland Islands English

This point is exemplified by the English of the Falkland Islands (see further Trudgill, forthcoming), one of a number of colonial Englishes currently spoken in the southern hemisphere. English has been spoken by settlers in the Falkland Islands since the middle of the nineteenth century, which is about the same length of time that English has been spoken by sizeable numbers of speakers in New Zealand. Unlike New Zealand, however, the Falklands were settled by very few people indeed (current population c. 2000), with many of them living to this day in isolated, scattered settlements. A consequence of this is that many of the settlements, particularly on West Falkland, have retained dialects of English which reflect the area of origin of the first settlers, with some villages speaking what is basically west country English, and so on (Tom Melchionne, personal communication). Very little mixing has taken place, and very little focusing. An exception to this pattern, however, is provided by the capital, Port Stanley (population c. 1000). Here a new, relatively focused dialect *has* arisen over the last century and a half. Interestingly, moreover, the Port Stanley variety of English resembles rather closely the other southern hemisphere varieties of English, and one frequent report is that Port Stanley speakers 'sound like Australians'. Clearly, in the larger settlement there has been greater scope for the mixing of different British dialects, and for new-dialect formation. (Falkland Islands English does also show a little influence of *language* contact, with, for example, a number of loan-words from Spanish in the field of horse breeding and riding (see Strange, 1973; Miller, 1978).)

Newfoundland

There are also interesting parallels between the English of the Falklands and that of Newfoundland. Newfoundland covers an enormous area and is rather sparsely populated, and although English has been spoken there by settlers since the early 1600s (and before that by migrant fishermen), it has often been noted that villages may differ markedly from one another linguistically. The two clearest sources of Newfoundland English are, without a doubt, the English of Ireland and that of the south-western counties of England. It is often said, moreover, that some settlements still speak what is basically Irish English and others what are basically south-western English dialects. This would not be too surprising, given the similarities with the Falklands situation: the distances between settlements, and the low level of population. However, Story et al. (1982) suggest that the picture is actually a little more complicated than this, and indicate that, at least in the twentieth century, a certain amount of mixing and levelling has taken place, especially in the region of St John's, the capital.

Features of modern Newfoundland English which are due to Irish English include:

(1) The grammatical construction of *to be after doing something* = *to have just done something* (see below, p. 150);
(2) /θ/ and /ð/ often do not contrast with /t/ and /d/, respectively;
(3) The use of clear [l] rather than dark [ɫ] post-vocalically;
(4) The use of habitual *be* versus non-habitual *is*, as in: *There bes games in it and there bes basketball* (Harris, 1984b).

Features which can specifically be traced to an origin in south-western England, particularly the area of Somerset, Hampshire, Dorset, Devon, and Cornwall, include:

(1) Present-tense *-s* for all persons of the verb, as in *I goes*;
(2) Unstressed standard English *him* may correspond to /ən~ŋ/;
(3) *I, he, she, we, they* function as objective forms if the pronouns are stressed, as in *I used to see they*;
(4) *He* and *she* are used to pronominalize inanimate count (but not mass) nouns, as in *the hammer . . . he*.

Mixing in Australian English

It is not only in areas such as the Falklands and Newfoundland, however, that the issue of dialect mixing is a problematical one. For example, English has been spoken in Australia (to any extent) for something less than 200 years. One would imagine, therefore, that in this relatively new dialect it would be a reasonably simple matter to disentangle the consequences of dialect mixture from those of other processes, and certainly a much less complex task than in the case of longer-established colonial varieties such as Irish or American English.

It emerges, however, that the assumption that Australian English (and presumably therefore also New Zealand and South African English) is in origin a mixed dialect is a controversial one. There is in the literature a view that Australian English was brought to Australia as an already formed and established variety. This view has been argued for by Hammarström (1980), who suggests that Australian English is simply unmixed nineteenth-century London English; and by Collins (1975), who argues that Australian English may be in origin a mixed dialect, but that any mixing that occurred took place in England rather than later.

These views do have some evidence in their favour, and we must consider them carefully. And we may note, first of all, that it is not unknown for isolated colonial varieties, spoken by small populations, to eventually be more conservative linguistically than the parent variety, as in the case of, for instance, Icelandic versus Norwegian. (For a very insightful account of *why* this should be so, see J. Milroy and L. Milroy, 1985.) Thus Hammarström's belief that essentially Australian English differs from modern London English because of changes that have occurred in the latter is plausible. And it is very easy, of course, to think of features in respect of which Australian English clearly is more conservative than English English. Consider, for instance, the pronunciation of items of the type *consume, presume* etc. with /š/ or /ž/, usual in Australia and once widespread in England but now very rare; and the pronunciation of *off* with /ɔː/ rather than /ɒ/, again old-fashioned in England but more current in Australia.

Let us begin to discuss the issue of mixing in Australian English by, for the moment, accepting part of Hammarström's premise – that Australian English arrived in Australia already intact – and ask ourselves the question: if Australian English is some form of nineteenth-century English, what sort of dialect is it? Where is it from – London, or somewhere else?

Clearly Australian English, like most of the other southern hemisphere varieties, particularly those of New Zealand and South Africa, is typologically *south of England* in origin. If one did not know of the existence of Australia, one would unhesitatingly assign an Australian accent to 'somewhere in the south-east of England'. Unlike north of England varieties, for example, Australian English has a system of six short vowels, with the vowels of *put* and *but* distinct. Unlike south-western varieties of English English, however, it is non-rhotic. We may bear in mind, moreover, that until recently the working-class dialects of all or most of the English counties of Kent, Sussex, Surrey, and Buckinghamshire, now predominantly non-rhotic, *were* rhotic. We would therefore suppose that the origins of Australian English lay in the type of English spoken in the nineteenth-century counties of Norfolk, Suffolk, Essex, Middlesex, eastern Hertfordshire, Cambridgeshire, eastern Northamptonshire, and eastern Bedfordshire, centring, of course, on London (see map 4.1).

If we now look at the modern dialects of these English areas, and particularly London, concentrating on phonetics and phonology, we observe that there are a number of characteristics of the region which might appear to cause difficulties for Hammarström's thesis, but which can be accounted for by arguing for the conservatism of Australian English.

(1) Accents of English in London and the Home Counties, as we saw in chapter 2, have a very strong tendency to total vocalization of [ɬ], with subsequent merger of many vowels in the environment before /l/, e.g. *fill*, *feel* [fɪʊ]. Australian English, on the other hand, is not widely recognized as having this feature.

However, it appears that *l* vocalization is a feature that has only very recently occurred in Home Counties accents, and is indeed still spreading very rapidly outwards from London. It is therefore very likely that in London also it for the most part postdated the beginnings of Australian English. And in any case, there actually are some tendencies to this development in Australian – and more especially New Zealand – English (see Trudgill and Hannah, 1982).

(2) The glottal-stop realization of /t/ as in *but* [bæ̈ʔ], *butter* [bæ̈ʔɐ] in

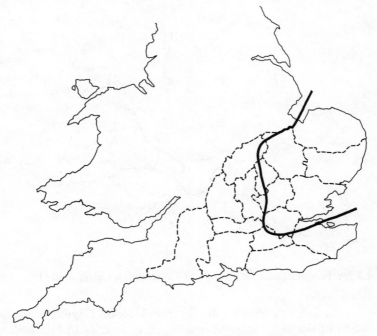

Map 4.1   Probable main area of origin of Australian English

London and neighbouring areas is very common indeed, but more or less unknown in Australian English, where final [t˺] or even [t~t‘] is usual. Once again, however, Wells (1982) and Andrésen (1968) show that the glottal stop is a relatively recent development in Britain and may, therefore, postdate the departure of English speakers for Australia. The Survey of English Dialects (Orton et al., 1962–71) lends some support to this view, showing [ʔ] in rural dialects only in northern East Anglia (see map 4.2).

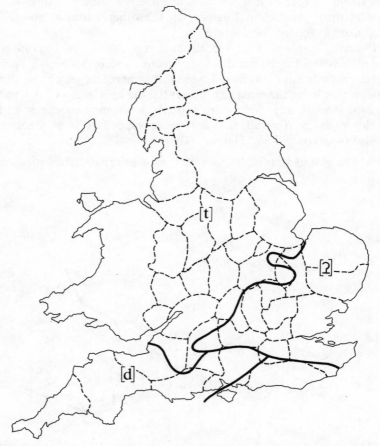

Map 4.2   /t/ in *water* (after Survey of English Dialects, Orton et al., 1962–1971)

(3) Australian English also differs from London English in the pronunciation of the short front vowels /ɪ/, /ɛ/ and /æ/ as in *bid*, *bed*, and *bad*:

	London	*Australia*
bid	[ɪ~i̠]	[i]
bed	[ɛ]	[e]
bad	[æ̠]	[ɛ]

It is true that the Cockney vowels tend to be closer than their counter-parts in RP, but the Australian variants are clearly and distinctively closer than those of Cockney (as are indeed /ɛ/ and /æ/ in New Zealand and South Africa also). A number of writers interpret these close front vowels as being a result of innovations that have taken place in Australian English of the type illustrated in figure 4.1 – and note that this suggests that New Zealand /ɪ/ = [ə] is at a more advanced stage of this change than even Australian English. For further discussion, see Bauer (1979).

However, we can note that the movement of these short vowels upwards in phonological space contradicts one of the principles established by Labov et al. (1972) – which is based, it is true, on a detailed examination of American English much more than any other variety or language – that it is 'tense' vowels that rise, and non-peripheral 'lax' (in this case, short) vowels that fall. Now, a case could be made out for arguing that /æ/ has become or is becoming 'tense', and this has led some scholars to believe that the non-natural move of /ɪ/ and /ɛ/ upwards in Australian English is simply a move forced on them in a push-chain sequence (Martinet, 1955). A much more reasonable account, however, is the following: Labov et al. are quite right to suppose that short vowels, at least in English, fall, not rise. Australian English, moreover, is not a counter-example. Just as in the case of [ɫ] and [ʔ], Australian English is at this point once again more *conservative* than London English, and not vice versa, and does indeed reflect nineteenth-century usage. The evidence for this is the following. We have already seen that a number of London features are currently spreading quite rapidly out into neighbouring areas (see also Trudgill, 1982). It is therefore possible that, in some cases, we can gain some idea of what London English used to be like by examining the dialects of neighbouring areas. We do not know, for instance, how /ɪ/ or /ɛ/ were pronounced in early-nineteenth

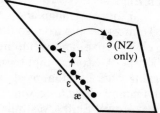

Figure 4.1   Innovations in Australian short front vowels

century London, but we *do* know how they were pronounced in the English of East Anglia (Norfolk, Suffolk, Essex) in the speech of people born in and around 1870, since the Survey of English Dialects (Orton et al., 1962–71) investigated precisely people of this age, and it is very likely that at least some features of the accent current in London in 1800 were still current in rural East Anglia in 1870. The phonetic transcriptions employed by the SED are not very helpful on this point, though, since they write [ɛ] for /ɛ/ over nearly the whole of England and give no phonetic details for /ɪ/ and /ɛ/ for East Anglia. Their tape recordings, however, as well as my own researches in East Anglia, add detail to the picture: older speakers in Norfolk, for example, to this day employ pronunciations such as *hill* [hil], *bed* [bed]. We can therefore propose a historical progression as follows, in accordance with the principles suggested by Labov et al. and taking, perhaps, the form of a drag-chain:

	stage			
	I	II	III	IV
bid	i	i	i	ɪ
bed	e	e	ɛ	ɛ
bad	ɛ	æ	æ	æ

Stage I is still found in Australian English. Stage II is typical of older, rural East Anglian speech. Stage III can be found in London, the area of Birmingham, and in some parts of the Falkland Islands. And stage IV is of course typical of modern RP.

A further comparison of modern Home Counties English with that of Australia produces some other features which appear to cause difficulties for Hammarström's thesis, but which can actually be explained as innovations in Australian English. It would obviously be naïve, that is, to regard colonial varieties as more or less static.

(1) One apparent difficulty for Hammarström is the case of the diphthongs of *bee, bay, buy, boy, boot, boat, bout*. Many descriptions of Australian English point out that these diphthongs are very wide – that is, there is a large phonetic distance between the first and the last elements – as in London English. It has to be emphasized, however, as Wells (1982) has done, that the Australian and London diphthongs are by no means identical. To most people from southern England, Australian diphthongs are very distinctive, and would never be confused with Cockney. The fact is that the Australian diphthongs are typically wider even than those of working-class London, as shown in table 4.1. Wells (1982) labels this phenomenon *diphthong shift*, and describes it as a continuation of the Great Vowel Shift, Australian English being more advanced than London English in this respect. He also explains this

phenomenon by claiming that Australian English (along with New Zealand and South African English) has taken this developing trend further than south-east of England varieties because it was freed from the restraining, conservative effect of RP in the convict settlement/ colonial situation.

Table 4.1 Diphthong comparisons

	RP	London	Australian
bee	ii	əɪ	ɜ·ɪ
bay	eɪ	æɪ	a̠·ɪ
buy	a̠ɪ	ɑɪ	ɒ·ɪ
boy	ɔɪ	ǫɪ	o·ɪ
boot	ʉu	ʏʉ	ʉ·ʉ˥
boat	ɵʊ	æ̞u	au
bout	ɑʊ	ɛu	æʉ

Source: Wells, 1982.

(2) We also have to note that there is a tendency for Australian English diphthongs not only to be wider than those in England but also to be *slower*, with the first element being emphasized more than the second, with a resultant tendency to monophthongization. This appears to be at its most advanced in South African English, where we have a historical progression of the type:

$$/aɪ/ = [a̠ɪ] > [ɑ̠i] > [ɑɪ] > [ɒɪ] > [ɒ·ɪ] > [ɒ·ˡ] > [ɒ·ə] > [ɒː]$$

The same tendency is clearly apparent in Australian English also, however, and especially in the 'broader' or more Australian varieties. This, too, has to be an independent development, since it is not at all in evidence in any English English variety (except that some forms of Cockney do have monophthongal variants of /au/ (=[a:]; see Gimson, 1980). It is, of course, of very considerable interest that all three main southern hemisphere varieties show signs of this tendency, but our major conclusion at this stage has to be that at least some of the phonological differences between Australian English and that of the putative south-east of England homeland – as more obviously in lexis – are due to changes that have occurred in Australia.

We now turn, however, to features of pronunciation that do cause genuine difficulties for Hammarström's thesis. These are features where innovation in either Australia or England seems unlikely, and where dialect mixture seems the most reasonable explanation.

(1) One of the most significant respects in which Australian English

differs from Cockney is in its treatment of unstressed vowels in words such as *horses, wanted, naked, village, David* etc. There is considerable variation in the way in which these vowels are realized in English English (see Wells, 1982), with, it is true, /ə/ very much on the increase at the expense of /ɪ/. The fact is, however, that London English typically has unstressed /ɪ/ in items of the above type, as in [dæɪvɪd], while Australian English typically has /ə/: [daˑˈvəd]. Linguistic change in Australian English cannot be entirely ruled out here, but the extent to which the /ə/ form is the norm in Australia strongly suggests that if we are to follow Hammarström in believing that Australian English is simply a nineteenth-century English dialect (plus some innovations), then that dialect cannot have been London English. We would have to look instead to an area which is, and was, quite similar to London linguistically but which has /ə/ rather than /ɪ/ in the relevant unstressed syllables. This would, in my view, have to be the East Anglian county of Essex. East Anglian dialects generally (see chapter 2) have /ə/ in the same environments as Australian English, and even educated speakers from these counties have /ə/ in items such as *hundred, wanted, horses* etc., though not in *David, naked*, etc., where /ə/ is today typical only of working-class and rural dialect speech (see map 4.3). (Norfolk and Suffolk can be excluded as a source for Australian English because, although they have Australian-style /ə/, they do not, or at least did not, have the wide diphthongs of London and Australia. We exclude the possibility here that London English underwent an innovation */ə/ > /ɪ/, on the grounds that there appears to have been for some while a clear trend in the other direction in most southern varieties: see Wells, 1982.)

(2) Another important feature which distinguishes modern Australian from London English and which points to mixing in Australian English concerns the vowel /ɑː/ of *bar, card* etc. London English has a back vowel [ɑː~ɒː] in these items, whereas Australian (and New Zealand) English have a very different and very distinctively front vowel [aː~æː]. Here again, Australian English agrees with the English of Essex and the rest of East Anglia, where front vowels also predominate, rather than with London.

These two phonological features suggest, then, that although there were probably very many similarities between nineteenth-century London English and Australian English, the two were by no means identical. In some respects, in fact, Australian English probably resembled more closely the English of Essex. It is highly unlikely, however, that Australian English actually *came from* Essex, particularly since, as Bernard (1969) and others have shown, there was a heavy preponderance of Londoners in the early Botany Bay colony. Much more reasonable would be a supposition that Australian English is indeed a mixed dialect, incorporating mainly London features but also including features from elsewhere in south-eastern England, including especially perhaps Essex.

If this is so, then clearly Hammarström's thesis is incorrect. But what of that of Collins? Collins (1975) has argued that Australian English *is* a mixed dialect, but that the mixing took place in the 'south-eastern quadrant of England', mainly in London and other towns, and that it involved, predominantly, southern and East Anglian dialects. We feel bound, as we have said, to agree with Collins that Australian English is indeed of mixed origin, and that the south and East Anglia are important in this mixture, especially in view of the predominance of

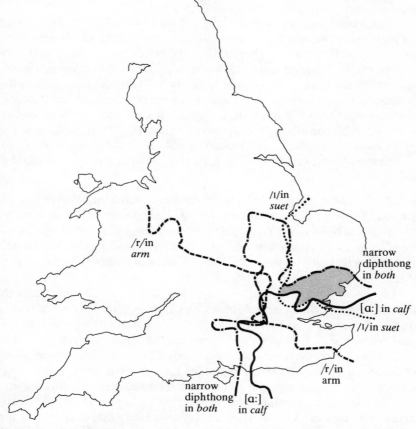

Map 4.3   Area of England which has [aː] in *calf*, no /r/ in *arm*, /ə/ in *suet*, and wide diphthongs in *both*, as in Australian English (after Survey of English Dialects, Orton et al., 1962–71)

unstressed /ə/. It is by no means clear, however, that this mixing did indeed occur on English soil. Features which make us feel uneasy about this suggestion include the following:

(1) Speakers in London, East Anglia, and the south of England generally have the /ɑ:/ vowel of *bar* etc. in the set of *laugh, path, pass* etc. and in the set of *dance, plant, sample* etc. They differ in this respect, of course, from the English midlands and north, which have the /æ/ of *bat* in these sets, and from Scotland and the English south-west, which do not have an /æ/–/ɑ:/ contrast. Australian English agrees with London English in mostly having /ɑ:/ before voiceless fricatives in the *laugh, path* set. But it *disagrees* with London English in having /æ/ in the set of *dance, plant* etc. in the speech of the majority, although there is some regional and social variation in this (see below).

This becomes much easier to explain if we allow, as ingredients in the mixture that went into the formation of Australian English, British Isles varieties which to this day do not have /ɑ:/ in *dance* etc. These varieties are: north of England dialects, which consistently have /æ/ in *dance*, and which have also contributed lexically to Australian English quite considerably (see Baker, 1966); and south-west of England and Scottish varieties which do not have an /ɑ:/ vowel at all – and which have also made a lexical contribution to Australian English. This in turn becomes much easier to account for – indeed, it only really becomes *possible* to account for it – if we allow for at least some dialect mixing in Australia itself.

(2) Australian English differs dramatically from most varieties of English English in its treatment of /h/. The whole of south-eastern England has been *h*-less (see chapter 2) for a long time, and pronunciations such as [æʔ] *hat* are entirely usual in London and elsewhere. Australian English, on the other hand, is basically *h*-pronouncing: *hat* is [hɛt].

One obvious explanation for this that would be compatible with Collins's thesis would be, once again, the influence, in a dialect mixture, of the dialects of Essex and elsewhere in East Anglia which are, as we saw in chapter 2, traditionally *h*-pronouncing. This, however, will not do as a total explanation, since we actually have a considerable amount of evidence to suggest that Australian English *used to be h-less*. The evidence is, first, that working-class Australian English still has a vestigial amount of *h*-dropping (see Wells, 1982). Inner-city Sydney teenagers, for instance, occasionally employ pronunciations such as [it] for *hit*. Secondly, it is clear from the work of Gordon (1983; see also Gordon and Deverson, 1985) that the closely related New Zealand English, similarly devoid of *h*-dropping today, formerly had a strong tendency to *h*-lessness. Gordon quotes, for example, from a school inspector who, writing in 1884, says that 'The initial "h" is cruelly neglected in many quarters.' South African English, too, although today showing no sign of *h*-dropping, was probably also *h*-less in previous generations. The expert on South African English, L. W. Lanham, who has researched diaries and letters of 1830s South Africans, writes (personal communication) 'I am convinced that *h*-dropping was widespread among the Settlers.'

The problem thus becomes one of accounting for the presumably gradual but almost total disappearance of *h*-dropping from modern Australian English. The efforts of diligent school teachers alone seem unlikely to provide an explanation, since their not notably less diligent counterparts in England and Wales have had absolutely no success in eradicating *h*-dropping. Neither does the influence of RP speakers seem likely to have been important, since we have already noted that it was precisely their lack of influence that speeded the process of diphthong shift. What we cannot ignore is that there was one big difference between nineteenth-century Australia and London, namely that present in Australia during that time were not only (variably) *h*-less Londoners and south-easterners, but also entirely *h*-ful Irish and Scottish speakers of English (as well as East Anglians, RP speakers, and speakers from a few other small *h*-ful areas of England).

It has been usual to discount the influence of bilingual or monolingual speakers of Irish English in the formation of Australian and other colonial varieties of English (see Turner, 1966; and the *Macquarie* dictionary). The fact is, however, that very large numbers of people indeed were sent, directly or indirectly, from Ireland to Australia, and for many decades they provided a sizeable proportion of the population there. From what we have learned in previous chapters, moreover, it seems that it is likely that, even if they were always a minority, they will have had some linguistic influence on the newly emerging mixed dialect *if* the processes involved in accommodation favoured the retention of features of their speech. We cannot assume that, just because Irish English was *present* in Australia, it necessarily had any role in new-dialect formation. But if both the demographic and linguistic factors were right, some influences will have been felt.

In fact, the evidence that Irish English played a role in the formation of Australian English, if perhaps a small one, is rather strong – and evidence at the grammatical and lexical levels gives us confidence about some of our more speculative suggestions at the phonological level. At the grammatical level we can point to:

(1) The presence in non-standard Australian English of the second-

person plural pronoun *youse*. As we have seen, this is unknown in most of England, and is almost entirely confined there to the vicinity of Liverpool and Newcastle, where Irish influence has been very heavy (see Beal, forthcoming). In Scotland it is most common in Glasgow, for the same reason. It is, on the other hand, very common indeed in Ireland, and for many speakers is absolutely categorical (see chapter 2).

(2) The grammatical construction exemplified in *Come here till I kiss you* (= so that I can kiss you) is not known, or even understood, in England – except, again, in Liverpool. It is, however, very usual in Ireland (and in the west Highlands of Scotland). It is not a part of standard Australian English, but it is well known to many Australians as a non-standard form.

(3) The adverbial usage of *but* as in *I don't want it but.* is common in Australia, Scotland, and Ireland, but is unknown in England apart from in the far north-east.

(4) Perhaps the most convincing grammatical evidence for the influence of Irish English is the following. In Australian English, a very frequent negative form of epistemic *must* is *must not/mustn't*. Very many Australians would say, for instance: *He mustn't have see me – he didn't stop.* This form is unknown in standard English English and in the vast majority of regions of England, where the usual negative forms of epistemic *must* is *can't* (see Quirk et al., 1972), as in: *He can't have seen me.* The one exception in England is in the north-west, around Liverpool, and in Newcastle, where *mustn't* is also usual. This in itself, of course, points quite clearly to an input into Australian English from somewhere other than the south-east of England. More particularly, however, negative epistemic *mustn't* is also the usual form in almost all varieties of Irish English (hence its presence in Liverpool). This is especially clear evidence for the role of Irish English in the development of Australian English, since an origin in England for this feature is obviously out of the question.

(5) The northern Irish usage of *whenever* to refer to a single occasion is known to some Australian and, especially, New Zealand speakers, as in *Whenever I was born, my parents were very poor.*

(6) The usage in colloquial Australian English of *It is so* as a denial (cf. American English *It is too*) contrasts with English English usage, where the majority form is simply *It is*. It is identical with the usage in (at least) northern Ireland (and Scotland), however.

As far as lexis is concerned, there is some dispute as to Irish influence, but some writers refer to Australian English *larrikin* 'rascal' as having Irish English origins – an Irish pronunciation of *lark* is sometimes cited.

Similarly, *nick* 'steal' and *purler* 'fall' (see Baker, 1966) are sometimes said to be of Irish origin, as is, of course, the well-known, if by now a little outdated, Australianism *sheila* 'girl', although this, too, has alternative etymologies.

And as far as pronunciation is concerned, we note the following important points:

(1) As we saw above, although most south-east of England accents have unstressed /ɪ/ in items such as *naked*, Australian English has /ə/. It is therefore of some considerable significance that Irish English normally has /ə/ in this lexical set. As Wells (1982, p. 427) points out, in Irish English '*abbot* and *rabbit* rhyme perfectly, both with one another and, usually, with *grab it*, all /-æbət/.' Compare this with Wells's (1982, p. 602) description of Australian English where, equally, '*pack it* is . . . homophonous with *packet*, both /pækət/.'

(2) Australian English does not have pre-glottalization or glottaling of word-final /p/, /t/, /k/. This distinguishes it sharply from London English, where glottalization (see Wells, 1982, p. 324) is the norm. The absence of this feature in Australia may well be due to its being a late-nineteenth-century innovation in London. It may also be, however, that the Australian tendency actually to release word-final /p,t,k/, often together with some aspiration, is due to the influence of certain British Isles varieties. Accents which release and/or aspirate word-final voiceless plosives, without glottalization, are found today in the West Midlands of England, Wales, Liverpool, and Ireland. In Liverpool, indeed, word-final /p,t,k/ may actually be [ɸ, ṱ, x], where [ṱ] is, according to Wells, an ungrooved tongue-tip fricative distinct from [s]. Wells also points out (1982, p. 372) that 'this frication of plosives has its parallel in the [ṱ] of Irish English', and, as we have seen, Liverpool English does undoubtedly owe much of its distinctiveness to heavy Irish immigration. (On Irish [ṱ] see further Hickey, 1984.) Australian English does not, of course, have actual frication, but, especially in the speech of women, the aspiration of word-final /p,t,k/ represents a striking difference from most English and Scottish variants.

As far as the influence of Scottish English in the formation of southern hemisphere varieties is concerned, we can note the presence in Australian English of Scottish vocabulary such as *whinge* 'whine', *bisom* 'bad child', *skite* 'hit', *billy* 'can' (see Baker, 1966) and *jink* 'play truant'. We can note, further, the presence in New Zealand English of constructions such as *Will I turn on the light?*, which is unknown in England, where *shall* or *should* are used, but normal in Scotland. And some phonological characteristics of New Zealand English can be ascribed to both Irish and Scottish influence, such as the strong tendency to preserve [ʍ] in *which* etc.; the presence of rhotic accents in the southern part of South Island; and the realization of /ɪ/ with a Scottish-type central vowel [ə] (see below).

We assume, then, that Australian (with probably also New Zealand and South African) English, although predominantly south-east of England in character, and although naturally having undergone independent linguistic changes, is a mixed dialect which grew up in Australia out of the interaction of south-eastern English forms with East Anglian, Irish, Scottish and other dialects. This is also the point of view espoused by Blair (1975), who writes that his evidence suggests that 'the amalgamation of British dialects as a basis for Australian pronunciation was completed in the colonies rather than in London.' His evidence is taken from an examination of early printed materials up to 1855. Dixon (1822), for example, talks in connection with Australia of 'the amalgamation of such various dialects assembled together', while Gerstaecker (1853) writes that 'the broad Irish brogue and the London Cockney dialect seemed to strike me everywhere.'

Interdialect in Australia

If Australian English and the other forms of colonial English are in origin mixed varieties, we should find in these dialects, as in Høyanger, evidence of interdialect forms, levelling, simplification, and other processes. Is this in fact the case?

As far as *interdialect forms* are concerned, Australian English does provide a few possible candidates for the label of *intermediate form*. For example, in the English of the British Isles, we can note the following different realizations of /r/: [r] in Scotland and parts of northern England; [ɽ] in Ireland and south-western England; [ɹ] the rest of England; and [ʋ] in the areas around London. The [ʋ] variant is probably very recent, and was therefore not involved in the Australian mixture process. Of the others, we can suppose that the heavily retroflexed approximant [ɽ] and the alveolar continuant [ɹ] were the most important. It is therefore of considerable interest to notice that a very widespread realization of /r/ in Australian English is a continuant that is *lightly* retroflexed. This may, of course, simply be a more conservative, earlier London-area pronunciation, but it is equally likely to be a phonetic compromise – a form, arising through contact, which is phonetically intermediate between Irish English [ɽ] and London English [ɹ].

Levelling in southern hemisphere English

As far as *levelling* is concerned, we can note that, as in Høyanger, forms that occur in a majority of the contributing dialects win out and survive in the emerging focused dialect, as a result of 'accommodating out' (see chapter 3). This might be a partial explanation, for instance, for the presence of /h/ in Australian English:

Cockney	S. E. England	E. Anglia	RP	Ireland	Scotland	Australia
Ø	Ø	/h/	/h/	/h/	/h/	/h/

(We note also the *salience* of the opposition /h/ vs. ø.) Clearly, it will also help a form to survive, however, if, as we have seen in earlier chapters, it is unmarked, with the more marked variants being levelled out. Consider, for example, the presence of /ə/ in the set of *naked*, *village* etc. in Australian English:

Cockney	S. E. England	RP	E. Anglia	Ireland	Australia
/ɪ/	/ɪ/	/ɪ/	/ə/	/ə/	/ə/

Here the unmarked, neutral mid-central vowel is the one to survive.

Bearing in mind then that by *levelling* we indicate a process whereby, in a dialect mixture situation, those elements disappear which are marked either universally *or* in terms of the particular language undergoing koinéization, we can point to the following features which characterize Australian English as being a levelled variety:

(1) The great similarity of Australian English to other southern hemisphere English varieties, and particularly that of New Zealand;

(2) The general character of Australian English as belonging very much to the 'mainstream' of English varieties, without any unusual or exotic characteristics to provoke comment on the part of English-speaking lay-persons or excite interest on the part of dialectologists; and

(3) The much-reported extreme uniformity of Australian English.

On the first point we can note that while, naturally, Australasians on the one hand and English-speaking South Africans on the other have no difficulty at all in distinguishing between their different accents, very many British people do have difficulty in telling a South African from, say, a New Zealander, particularly if the accents are not of the 'broad' variety. Most British people, moreover, including distinguished academic English-language scholars, have *very* great difficulty in distinguishing between Australian and New Zealand accents of English. The similarities between the three main southern hemisphere varieties –

some of them shared by Falkland Islands English – that cause these problems include:

wide diphthongs, the products of diphthong shift;
slow diphthongs, with a tendency to monophthongization;
high short front vowels.

A number of explanations could be advanced to account for these similarities:

(1) We could say, with Hammarström, that all the southern hemisphere varieties are simply nineteenth-century London English, plus some independent developments.
(2) Alternatively we could suggest, with Collins, that the varieties descend from a mixed south-east of England variety which was formed before colonization.
(3) We can agree with Wells (1982) that the colonial varieties all continue trends already present in England but slowed down by the inhibiting influence of RP.
(4) We could also, in discussing the great similarity of Australian and New Zealand English, note the role played by Australians in the settlement of New Zealand.

Some or all of these explanations may be relevant. But it is actually more likely to be the case that the similarities arise from dialect mixture processes that took place, as Blair (1975) argues for Australia, in the colonies themselves. If the British Isles varieties that went into the initial dialect mixture processes were roughly the same for all southern hemisphere countries, and in approximately the same proportions, then it is not surprising if the *output* of the mixture is roughly the same in each case. This is particularly likely to be so if it is true, as we have suggested above, that the same universal or at least widespread levelling tendencies were at work in each of the dialect contact situations. (The character of Port Stanley English – see p. 128 – strengthens this view.) In so far as the three major varieties are *different*, then this can be accounted for by *differences* in the input to the mixture together with, of course, later developments, and the influence of other languages (notably Afrikaans in South Africa).

As far as the character of Australian, New Zealand, and South African English as 'mainstream' varieties is concerned, we can readily explain this again in terms of levelling. If unusual, exotic, marked features are removed during the koinéization associated with new-dialect formation, then it is hardly surprising if all these new dialects have few unusual, exotic, marked features. And it is certainly true that most of the linguistic forms found in, say, Australian English, particularly as far as core phonology and grammar are concerned, are also found in most or at least many other varieties of English. There are few exotica in Australian English, and it actually, even in its non-standard varieties, more closely resembles standard English English than do most of the non-standard dialects found in the British Isles themselves. We do not find, in Australian English, the /x/ of Scots, or the [ʀ̥] of Northumberland. Nor do we find anything resembling the verb system of American Black Vernacular English, or the aspectual distinctions of south-western England. Obviously, the more common a feature was in the English varieties of the British Isles, the more frequently it was likely to occur in the colonial mixture situation, and the more likely it therefore was to survive in Australian English. Those exotic features which occurred in only a few dialects were unlikely, for demographic reasons, to survive, although as we argued above, linguistically unmarked minority forms (such as /ə/) had a better than average chance of being retained.

This characteristic of southern hemisphere Englishes as levelled varieties is also shared by most other forms of colonial English. In Britain, for example, the English of the Scottish Highlands, north Wales, and western Cornwall are notable for being non-dialectal. And, as Wells (1982) has pointed out, divergent traditional dialects are found nowhere outside the British Isles (unless perhaps in the American Appalachians and the Canadian Maritimes). Elsewhere, varieties which diverge markedly from mainstream English owe their characteristics to language contact and pidginization/creolization.

As far as the third point is concerned, the extreme uniformity of Australian English has been much remarked on. This uniformity appears to be quite typical of the initial stages of mixed, colonial varieties (cf. Canada, below), with degree of uniformity being in inverse proportion to historical depth. It can be explained partly – as we explained the similarities between all three major southern hemisphere varieties – in terms of levelling, dialect mixture, and similar ingredients. We also have to note, however, the role of settlement patterns and population movements. As Bernard (1969) has pointed out, the first white Australians came into the country through a small number of seaports, and kept in contact by sea through these same ports.

It is interesting to note, however, that the relatively new, mixed, uniform Australian variety is now showing definite signs of beginning to develop regional differentiation – although many of these signs are apparent only after detailed linguistic analyses. Bradley (1981) cites, for example, the pronunciation of *tour* as [tʰɔ̞:] in the Sydney area, as opposed to [tʰʊə] elsewhere; and the Sydney realization of /u:/ as in *food* as [ʉu], as opposed to the [uʉ] of Melbourne and Adelaide. Bradley also notes that /ɪ/, /ɛ/, and /æ/ tend to be closer in Melbourne than elsewhere, while /ʊ/ and /ɒ/ have less marked lip-rounding there than elsewhere. It is probable that, given time, differences of this type will increase, giving rise eventually to instantly recognizable varieties. Australians have traditionally claimed to recognize the origins of their compatriots only from lexical clues. Younger Australians, however, are now very often able to use phonetic evidence to locate speakers in a negative way, saying, for example, 'I don't know where she's from, but she's not from here.' Perhaps in another 100 years' time, positive identifications will have become possible.

Levelling in Canadian English

Similar developments are reported from another colonial variety of English, that of Canada. Chambers and Hardwick (1985) report a very high degree of homogeneity in inland Canadian English. The levelling that occurred during colonization has led to the growth of a more or less homogeneous variety which is spoken from Ontario right to the west coast. This, however, is true only as far as urban, middle-class speech is concerned. In describing a situation which reminds us that, as in Newfoundland, transplantation does not necessarily lead to mixing, Chambers and Hardwick write: 'Inland rural dialects often differ sharply from standard speech, especially in the numerous rural communities in which the founders were Irish and Scots, and inland working-class dialects differ not only from standard speech but also from one another, with the ethnic origins of the founders cutting across social class.' Note that this description indicates a sharp distinction between Canada and Australia, where linguists are prepared to acknowledge that rural varieties differ from urban varieties, *but not from each other*.

The great homogeneity of middle-class, urban Canadian English can be ascribed to the rapid spreading, from 1870 onwards, of the already homogeneous southern Ontario dialect to the rest of central and western Canada as the country expanded. Regional variation, however, as in Australia, is now beginning to appear even in urban speech. Chambers and Hardwick's comparison of the English of Toronto and Vancouver, two cities over 2000 miles apart, now shows that, while they are remarkably similar, the dialects of the two cities are beginning to diverge somewhat. For example, in the diphthong /ɑu/ of *out* (see further below), younger Vancouver speakers are beginning to show a tendency to use variants with a rounded first element [ou]. Toronto, on the other hand, shows no trace of this at all. Once again, as in Australia, we notice that differences are so far only of a fine phonetic type. We may predict, however, that in years to come these differences will increase in number and degree.

Simplification in colonial English

We have clear evidence, then, from at least some varieties of colonial English, of mixing and of levelling. We now, therefore, turn our attention to the process of simplification, which we also know to occur during dialect contact and koinéization, as a result of imperfect accommodation. One of the problems here, however, is that, as we saw in the case of transplanted varieties of Hindi, simplification may be due to language contact rather than dialect contact: imperfect accommodation by adults is obviously even more likely to occur in the former than in the latter situation. As far as colonial varieties of English are concerned, this problem of analysis is probably most likely to arise in the case of the English of the United States. While native speakers of English have long been in a large majority in the USA, it is highly likely that the learning of English as a foreign language by millions of adult immigrants to America has had some influence on the language.

A comparison of US English with that of England suggests a number of candidates for the label of simplification, bearing in mind that this implies, for the most part, regularization. Let us look at some of these in turn.

(1) The most widespread past-tense forms in British English of verbs such as *burn, learn, dream, lean* etc. are *burnt, learnt, dreamt, leant* etc. These are irregular in that they add final *-t* and, in the case of *dream* and *lean*, involve a vowel change also. The most widespread forms in American English, on the other hand, are the entirely regular *burned, learned, dreamed, leaned* etc. Regularization of this type is a clear example of simplification and, as we saw in Høyanger, is of a type that we would expect to find in post-dialect-contact varieties. The number of verbs which tend to be irregular in Britain but regular in the USA is rather large, and would include, in addition: *dwell, smell, spell, spill, spoil, kneel, leap*. We must also acknowledge, however, that there are some verbs, such as *fit* and *dive*, which may have irregular past-tense forms (*fit, dove*) in US English but not in Britain.

(2) There is a very strong trend in American English to regularize the behaviour of semi-modals and auxiliaries by bringing them into line with other verbs. This trend can be observed in British English also, but to a much weaker extent. Compare:

British	*American*
He used not to go.	He didn't used to go.
Need you do it?	Do you need to do it?
Dare I do it?	Do I dare do it?
Have you any money?	Do you have any money?
etc.	etc.

(3) It is possible that the greater preponderance in American English of forms such as *I like to skate*, *I hate to swim*, which in British English would be more likely to be *I like skating*, *I hate swimming*, is mixture-induced simplification, removing a minority syntactic form (cf. *I want to go* and **I want going*). But, of course, this is also a clear candidate for being regarded as the result of the influence of European languages, rather than of dialect contact.

At the level of phonology, it is also interesting to note that at a number of points in the system of vowels and consonants, American English has undergone more *mergers* than varieties in Britain. As we saw in chapter 3, mergers almost always win out over distinctions in contact situations, as a result of simplification:

(1) The merger of the vowels of *cot* and *caught*, unknown in England (although usual in Scotland), is the norm in Canada, and is spreading with great rapidity in most areas of the USA.

(2) In most of North America away from the east coast – which is to say in those areas where the further mixing of already mixed dialects has taken place – there has been very considerable merging of vowels before /r/ in polysyllabic words, so that:

> *mirror* rhymes with *nearer*
> *merry*, *Mary*, *marry* are homophonous
> *hurry* rhymes with *furry*
> *hoary* and *horrid* have the same first syllable.

(3) The consonants /t/ and /d/ are merged in post-tonic intervocalic position as [ɾ~d], making homophones of *ladder*, *latter* (see chapter 1).

In each case, mergers such as these will reflect the long-term effect of individual speakers with a phonological contrast having less difficulty accommodating to speakers without a contrast than vice versa.

The problem of language contact

The degree to which simplification in American English is due to language contact rather than dialect contact (or indeed independent development) is clearly a difficult and possibly insoluble problem. Indeed, as we have already noted, it is often hard when dealing with colonial Englishes generally to distinguish between these two processes, the exception being mainly in areas which were previously uninhabited, such as the Falklands, or where native speakers of English heavily outnumbered others, as in New Zealand. Other transplanted languages, like Hindi, present the same difficulty, as we have seen.

One variety of colonial English in which the role of language contact has been regarded as controversial is Irish English. Irish English is, of course, one of the very oldest of the colonial English varieties, having been introduced into Ireland in medieval times and then, after having died out in most areas, being reintroduced from the seventeenth century onwards (see Bliss, 1984; Ó Muirithe, 1977). The last 300 years have then seen a process of almost total language shift, with relatively few English-Irish bilinguals remaining, and hardly any – perhaps no – Irish monolinguals.

It would be surprising if this process of language contact and language shift had not left any traces. And, unlike the American situation, where many languages have been involved, the effects of language contact in Ireland should be easier to detect, since only Irish and English were involved. Nevertheless, the role of Irish in the formation of Irish English remains controversial.

As an illustration of the difficulties involved in distinguishing between the effects of dialect and language contact, we turn now to a discussion of the work of Harris (1984b). Harris points out that the verb system of vernacular Irish English differs markedly and in a complex manner from that of English English, especially the standard variety, at a number of points. The problem is one of explaining the source of these differences and, in particular, of deciding whether they are due to the fact that Irish English is a colonial variety and/or the fact that it is in origin a second-language variety of English demonstrating interference from Irish. (For a study of the interaction of Irish with Canadian English, see Pringle, 1981.)

One area where vernacular varieties of Irish English are strikingly at odds with English English concerns the use of the perfect, which is very rare in vernacular Irish English. Corresponding to English English perfect verb forms, Irish English has instead different constructions which fulfil the same function, depending on precisely what that function is. These constructions are the following:

(1) If a transitive verb has *resultative* meaning, referring to a past event with present relevance, then it has a distinctively Irish English construction as in (a) *She's nearly her course finished.* There is also a stative resultative construction, which is confined to mutative intransitive verbs such as *change*, *die*, *go*, as in (b) *I'm not too long left.*

(2) If the verb has *indefinite anterior* reference, relating to 'an event occurring at an unspecified point in a period leading up to the present' (Harris, 1984b, p. 308), then Irish English uses the preterite, and relies on adverbials to differentiate between this

usage and past anterior (or 'then-time'), as in *I never saw a gun in my life*.

(3) If the verb is employed with what can be labelled a *hot-news* perfect function, as in *A young man has just got shot*, then Irish English employs another distinctive construction, as in *A young man's after getting shot*.

(4) If the English English perfect verb has an *extended-now* meaning, as in *We've lived here seventeen years*, then Irish English employs the present: *We're living here seventeen years*.

Forms such as these are often ascribed to substratum influence from Irish, which has no real perfect, and indeed Harris agrees that (3) is clearly a calque on Irish:

Irish:	Tá	sí	tréis	an	bád	a dhíol
	be+non-past	*she*	*after*	*the*	*boat*	*selling*

Irish English: She is after selling the boat.
English English: She has (just) sold the boat.

This form is not, and has not, been found anywhere in English other than Ireland and places such as Newfoundland and the Ottawa Valley, Canada, which were settled from Ireland.

In spite of the claims of other scholars, however, Harris argues convincingly that forms (1)(a), (1)(b), (2), and (4) are not – or not only – the result of the influence of Irish. Rather, they result from the fact that Irish English, like other colonial varieties, is in some respects linguistically conservative. Indeed, because of its origins in seventeenth-century English, it is dramatically more conservative at some points than most other later colonial varieties. The fact is, Harris shows, that all the Irish English forms except the *after* construction are retentions from Early Modern English.

For example, the resultative form (1)(a) may resemble to some extent the Irish construction:

Irish:	Tá	an	bád	díolta	aici
	be+non-past	*the*	*boat*	*sold*	*at-her*

Irish English: She has the boat sold.
English English: She has sold the boat.

But it also corresponds exactly to seventeenth-century English forms such as: '*Have you the lion's part written?*' (Shakespeare, *Midsummer Night's Dream*).

Similarly, the indefinite anterior form (2) has parallels in Irish:

Irish:	Chuaigh	sé	amach
	go+past	*he*	*out*

Irish English: He went out.
English English: He has gone out.

But it also corresponds to Middle English and, to an extent, Early Modern English, as well as American English and Scottish English, which are more conservative than English English in this respect and often prefer the preterite, as in *I never saw a gun in my life*, to the perfect *I have never seen . . . .*

Equally, the *extended-now* usage as in (4) has parallels in Irish:

Irish:	Tá	sé	marbh le	fada	riamh
	be+non-past	*he*	*dead with*	*long-time*	*ever*
Irish English:	He's dead a long time.				
English English:	He's been dead a long time.				

But, once again, Harris is able to point to uses of extended-now present-tense forms in Early Modern English, as in the Shakespearean sentence: 'Since the youth of the Count's was today with my Lady, she is much out of quiet.' (*Twelfth Night*)

Harris therefore concludes of Irish English that 'The non-standard distribution of . . . forms *vis-à-vis* the standard perfect appears to reflect Early Modern English patterns. The effects of Irish interference on the latter can perhaps best be regarded as reinforcing and indirect.' Multiple causation, that is, is acknowledged, but the conservatism of Irish English is seen as a more important explanatory factor than is the role of language contact. Clearly, however, it is difficult to be absolutely sure about relative strength of influence.

Harris also points out that dialect contact between vernacular Irish English and standard English has led to the growth, as we saw in chapter 3 in the case of St Kitts and Nevis, of a social dialect continuum between these two varieties. In view of the complex nature of the semantico-grammatical differences between standard and Irish English that we have just been discussing, we are not surprised to notice that the same contact that led to the continuum has also given rise to the development of intermediate and interdialect forms, such as:

Irish English	*standard English*	*interdialect*
I did it before.	I've done it before.	I've done it before.
They were here before.	They've been here before. →	They've been here before.
		↓
I did a course two years ago.	I did a course two years ago.	I've done a course two years ago.
They were here when we came.	They were here when we came.	They've been here when we came.

Sentences such as *I've done a course two years ago*, attested by Harris for some vernacular Irish English speakers, are clearly the result of *hyperadaptation*. We see once again interaction between dialects producing interdialect forms which originally occurred in neither. As Harris says, speakers who produce such forms have 'acquired the standard perfect *form* but less than complete control of its *function*'.

We may also note one further example of interdialect involving dialect contact and vernacular Irish English verb forms. As we have seen, Irish English has a hot-news perfect function for constructions such as *She's after selling the boat*. In Newfoundland, as we have already noted, this form is also widely employed. However, this construction has spread, through dialect contact, from basically Irish dialects to others which are basically English English in origin (see above). In acquiring this form, however, these dialects have extended its function to include relatively remote past events as well as hot-news. That is, they use the Irish English form in a hyperadaptive, non-Irish-English manner.

Reallocation in colonial English

We now return to an examination of those aspects of the koinéization of colonial Englishes in which we can be reasonably sure that we are dealing with the results of dialect contact and dialect mixture alone. It will be recalled that in the koinéized Bhojpuri of Mauritius, forms that were regionally distributed in the original Bhojpuri of India in some cases survive as stylistic variants. Reallocation of this type can be found also, as we would expect if we are dealing with originally mixed dialects, in transplanted varieties of English. One example of this is provided by the case of intervocalic /t/, as in *city*, which is realized in modern Britain as [t], [ʔ] or [ɾ~d̪] (see map 4.2). As we have already seen, there is considerable evidence that the [ʔ] variant is actually a relatively new pronunciation, and that it post-dates, as a British linguistic innovation, the formation of most colonial varieties. Of the two other variants, however, [ɾ~d̪] is typical of the rural dialects of south-western England, as map 4.2 shows, and also of some urban areas: Wells (1982) writes of 'the use of a voiced tap in words such as *butter* . . . which is certainly very common in urban areas such as Bristol'. The [t] variant occurs in the rest of the country, apart from in those localities which have [ʔ]. Both [ɾ~d̪] and [t] are clearly *regional* variants in Britain.

In certain colonial varieties, however, reallocation of these variants has taken place. While, say, most Americans use [d̪] and most Highland Scots use [t], most Australian English speakers have both variants in their repertoires. The variants, moreover, are stylistic alternants, with [t] being used in more formal styles, while in more informal styles [d̪] becomes increasingly likely. Wells (1982) writes of Australian English that 'intervocalic /t/ may undergo T-voicing, though it is perhaps more accurately described as *variably* subject to leniting, i.e. to becoming [d̪].' (my italics)

We may similarly observe that colonial Englishes also demonstrate the occurrence of reallocation of variants as *social-class* alternants during dialect mixing. For example, the incidence of /æ/ and /ɑ:/ in the lexical set of *dance, grant, sample* is in England regionally determined (see map 4.4). Most English English accents have a contrast between /æ/ as in *Pam* and /ɑ:/ as in *palm*. However, southern and northern accents differ as to the incidence of /æ/ and /ɑ:/ in two different lexical sets (see chapter 1, and above, p. 138). In the south, original /æ/ has been lengthened to /ɑ:/ before the front voiced fricatives /f/, /θ/, and /s/, as in *laugh, path, grass*. This southern innovation is found in most southern hemisphere colonial varieties of English, but not in the northern hemisphere, for the most part. Similarly, original /æ/ has been lengthened to /ɑ:/ in southern England also before /mp/, /nt/, /ns/, /nd/, and /nč/, as in *sample, grant, dance, command, branch*. This change has been less successful, however, and there are many words in the set which retain /æ/, such as *ample, ant, romance, band*. This change has similarly not been transmitted to most of the northern hemisphere colonial varieties, but the /ɑ:/ vowel is usual in the appropriate lexical items in South African and New Zealand English. In Australian English, however, the situation is a complex one. Pronunciations such as *dance* /dæns/, associated in England with northern areas such as Newcastle, Liverpool, Nottingham, and Leeds, and pronunciations such as /dɑ:ns/, associated in England with southern areas such as London, Cambridge, and Brighton, are both found in Australia. To a certain extent they are distributed regionally, with /ɑ:/ being more common in south Australia, but everywhere in Australia the two variants have been reallocated socially. Hammarström (1980, p. 10) writes that while /æ/ is common in Australian English in words such as *chance*, it is 'sociolectally lower', and that 'higher sociolects' have /ɑ:/. Wells (1982) also writes that many Australians 'consider /ɑ:/ high-class, even indicative of affectation, pedantry, or snobbishness, as against the popular pronunciation with /æ/.' (See also Bähr, 1974, p. 277; Trudgill and Hannah, 1982, p. 16) We can assume that both /æ/ and /ɑ:/ were present in the original mix of dialects that was brought to Australia, and that, as focusing was taking place, both forms survived by acquiring social-class differentiating functions. We note once again, moreover, as we did in chapter 1, the *salience* of the /æ/–/ɑ:/ contrast, and recall our earlier hypothesis (chapter 3) that it may be *extra-strong* salience that inhibits reduction of variants, and therefore encourages reallocation.

Canadian Raising

It is well known that the phonology of Canadian English, a 'colonial variety' of English in our sense, is characterized by the phenomenon commonly labelled *Canadian Raising* (see chapter 1): in Canadian English the diphthongs /ai/ and /au/ have radically different allophones depending on whether or not they are followed by a voiceless consonant (see Joos, 1942). Thus, we find pronunciations such as *night* [nəɪt] and *out* [əut] contrasting with *time* [taim], *tie* [tai] and *loud* [laud], *now* [nau]. That is, in the environment before a voiceless consonant, the diphthongs have a mid-central first element, giving rise to the label 'raising', while elsewhere they have an open first element. The phenomenon is well known not to be exclusively Canadian (see Chambers, 1979), since there are a number of areas in the USA, notably in Virginia and South Carolina, where it also occurs, although in these areas the phonetics is rather different. The phenomenon (see Chambers, 1979)

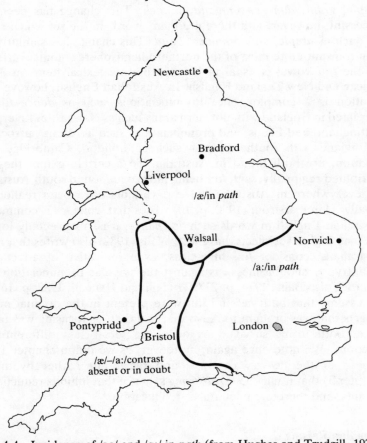

Map 4.4   Incidence of /ae/ and /ɑ:/ in *path* (from Hughes and Trudgill, 1979)

does not cover the whole of Canada, moreover, since some varieties of the English of Newfoundland and the Maritimes tend not to have it. It remains, however, a very distinctive feature of Canadian pronunciation, serving to differentiate it from other forms of North American English. The origins of Canadian Raising are intriguing, and a number of accounts of where, when, and why it arose are available. Let us examine the main contenders.

One obvious suggestion is that Canadian Raising is, diachronically speaking, not 'raising' at all but 'failure to lower'. This explanation would refer to the English Great Vowel Shift (GVS) and depend on the by now well-established fact that phonological changes frequently take place by spreading from one phonological environment to another. One well-investigated change of this type involves the phonetic raising of /æ/ in American English from [æ:] to [ɛ:] to [eə] and [ɪə]. In some northern US cities, the change has been completed in all environments; in others only before nasals, voiced stops and voiceless fricatives; in others only before nasals and voiced stops; and so on (see chapter 1). It is clear that there is a hierarchy of environments, with the change occurring first in the most favoured environments before spreading to others (see Bailey, 1973).

Given that we know that sound changes can occur in this way, it is perfectly possible that the Great Vowel Shift may also have taken place in this manner. It is perfectly possible, that is, that Middle English /u:/ gradually became /au/, through intermediate stages such as /ʊu/, /əu/, /ɜu/, and /ɐu/, with the opening of the diphthong starting earlier and progressing further in some environments than others. It also would be very understandable and natural if the wider diphthongs occurred in front of voiced consonants before they occurred in front of voiceless consonants. It is especially true of English, in most of its varieties, that vowels are longer in voiced than in voiceless environments. The wider diphthongs would therefore be more at home in voiced environments where there would be more milliseconds available for their articulation (see below). We can therefore postulate a scheme of the following type:

	/__[−voice]	/__ [+voice]
Middle English	u: *out*	u: *loud*
stage 1	u:	ʊu
stage 2	ʊu	əu
stage 3	əu	ɜu
stage 4	ɜu	ɐu
stage 5	ɐu	au
stage 6	au	au

One could then suggest that Canadian English, rather than taking the GVS to completion as in stage 6, has remained in a state of arrested development as in stage 5. Furthermore, once stage 5 had become symbolic of Canadian identity, there would be good reason for the shift never to go to completion in Canadian English by progressing to the stage 6 typical of the otherwise extremely similar American English. Canadian Raising, that is, represents a fossilization in this respect of an earlier stage of the language where the GVS has gone to completion only in the favoured environment.

There are two pieces of evidence, however, which argue against this interpretation, albeit not conclusively. One is that those areas of the southern USA which have the two widely differing allophones of /ai/ and /au/ have them as, for example: *night time* [nɔɪt taːm] (see Wells, 1982). That is, ME ī has an archaic pronunciation in the voiceless environments but an innovating pronunciation elsewhere, in which the GVS has been taken one stage further by monophthongization, [ai] > [aː]. There is no reason, of course, to believe that it is *necessarily* the case that a dialect cannot be both conservative and innovating, but it does make us just a little uncomfortable that the one environment has lagged so many stages behind the other in its development.

The other piece of evidence that we have to consider is the current situation in dialects of the British Isles. The fact is that ME ū, for example, can be found somewhere in the British Isles in every conceivable stage of its GVS development from /uː/ to /au/, such as:

out loud	uːt	luːd
	əʉt	ləʉd
	øyt	løyd
	ɛut	lɛud
	æʉt	læʉd
	ɜut	lɜud
	ɐʉt	lɐʉd
	ɑut	lɑud
	and so on	

(Some diphthongs, in fact, represent developments more advanced even than [ɑu].) The very striking fact, however, is that we nowhere find different allophones of /au/ in voiced and voiceless environments (see Orton et al., 1978). In the one small area where we do find different allophones of /ai/ (part of east Yorkshire), the phonetic forms bear no resemblance at all to Canadian Raising, being of the type *night time* [naɪt taːm]. It is odd, to say the least, that we have not been able to find preserved, somewhere in Britain, this putative earlier stage of the GVS, given that every other imaginable stage *is* to be found.

It must be admitted, of course, that Scottish English, including related northern Irish varieties, does demonstrate a phenomenon that looks, at first glance, very much like Canadian Raising, and which has been fully discussed by Gregg (1973). Recently, writers on Scots and Scottish English have come to call this phenomenon *Aitken's law* (see Aitken, 1984; Harris, 1984a), or the *Scottish Vowel Length Rule*. The fact is that most forms of Scots do have pronunciations such as *tight* [təɪt], *tied* [taɪd]. This, of course, is more or less identical to what one would expect to find in Canadian English. Unfortunately, however, Scots also usually has the pronunciation *tide* [təɪd], whereas Canadian English has [taɪd]. In actual fact, all vowels in Scots (where vowel length is not distinctive) have, with the exception of /ɪ/ and /ʌ/, longer pronunciations before /r/, voiced fricatives, and a morpheme boundary than they do elsewhere. Where a morpheme-final vowel is followed by another morpheme, moreover, the longer vowel remains unaffected. This gives rise to minimal pairs such as:

short	long
heed [hid]	he'd [hi:d]
brood [brʉd]	brewed [brʉ:d]
road [rod]	rowed [ro:d]

In the case of /aʼ̈i/, the short and long variants also vary in quality, as we have seen above. Comparison of Scots and Canadian English thus presents a number of points of difference:

	Scots	Canadian
tight	əɪ	əɪ
tide	əɪ - - - - - - -	aɪ
tied	aɪ	aɪ
fife	əɪ	əɪ
five	aɪ	aɪ
pipe	əɪ	əɪ
imbibe	əɪ - - - - - -	aɪ
ride	əɪ - - - - - -	aɪ
mile	əɪ - - - - - -. -	aɪ
line	əɪ - - - - - -	aɪ

Notice, moreover, that not only is this phenomenon confined to /ai/ in Scots, but that many of the morphophonemic alternations that occur in Canadian English are not found in many forms of Scots, e.g.:

	Scots	Canadian
wife	[wəɪf]	[wəɪf]
wives	[wəɪfs]	[waɪvz]
knife	[nəɪf]	[nəɪf]
knives	[nəɪfs]	[naɪvz]

Some might wish to argue that Canadian Raising may have arisen diachronically, as a Canadian innovation, as mixture-induced simplification of the Scottish Vowel Length Rule (cf. Gregg, 1973). Certainly it is simpler as far as the following consonantal environments are concerned (in Scots /v/, /z/, /ž/, /ð/, /r/ versus, in Canadian, all voiced consonants). But there remains the difficulty that in Scots /au/ does *not* have two different qualities even though it does have two different lengths. It is also worth noting that in many forms of Scots, /ai/ and /əi/ have become phonemically distinct (Aitken, 1984).

An alternative proposal is that provided by Chambers (1973, 1979). Chambers argues, in effect, that Canadian Raising is an innovation, the result of a linguistic change that occurred in heartland Canada. He then points out (1979), as we did above, that the change is a perfectly natural one, resulting from the shortening of vowels before voiceless consonants that occurs in most varieties of English:

> When the *shortening* rule was introduced into the grammar, it affected the low tense diphthongs particularly, since the 'distance' between the low onset and the peak of the upglide is greatest for these nuclei. As might be expected, some dialects consequently modify them in a manner that optimizes the distance . . . by raising the onset as in Canada and other areas where the Canadian Raising rule is found. Thus *Canadian Raising* originated as a reflex of the shortening rule.

In this view, of course, the term 'raising' is phonetically accurate not only synchronically but diachronically as well.

One of the strongest pieces of evidence in favour of this view comes from the recent work of William Labov on the English of Philadelphia (see Labov, 1983). Real-time studies show that whereas older speakers in the city have a low onset for /ai/ in all environments, there is now a very strong tendency for younger speakers to have a much more mid onset before *voiceless consonants only*. That is, for /ai/, though not for /au/, Canadian Raising, as a linguistic change, is just beginning to occur in Philadelphia.

We now propose a further explanation for the historical development of Canadian Raising. This explanation conflicts with the 'failure to lower' view, but not necessarily with the views of Gregg or Chambers described above. (In fact in sound change there are so many developments that *can* take place that, for a particular change *actually* to take place, there are very probably a *number* of factors working in its favour. Multiple causation, as we argued above, is always likely.)

This explanation stems from the analysis of heartland Canadian English as a mixed, colonial dialect. Indeed, we argue that Canadian English has Canadian Raising (partly) *because* it is a mixed dialect, and a relatively recent one at that. It could be argued against this, of course, that Canadian Raising does *not* occur in other colonial dialects of English, such as Australian English, so the proposed explanation is hardly valid. However, it is probable that Australian English, though mixed in origin, did not contain the right ingredients, or at least not in the right proportions. Moreover, there are actually *quite a large number* of other colonial Englishes where Canadian Raising *does* occur outside North America, as we shall see. (It is also possible to argue that those varieties of Canadian English which do not have Canadian Raising do not have it precisely because, as in the case of Newfoundland, they are not really mixed at all, or because, again, the ingredients were not right.)

We saw earlier (in chapter 3) that in Belfast English there is good reason to suppose that phonological differences between the contributing dialects in the initial dialect mixture led, during the process of variant reduction and focusing, to *allophonic variation*: in the case of /a/, those variants which were not lost were retained and *reallocated* according to phonological environment. Thinking along the same lines for Canadian English, we come up with the following analysis for Canadian Raising. Present in the mixture that preceded the formation of Canadian English were variants of /ai/ and /au/ from many different English, Scottish, Irish, and American varieties of English. Prominent among them were [əɪ]- and [əu]-type variants (in *night* and *time*, *out* and *loud*, respectively) of the type found in Scotland and parts of northern England, as well as [aɪ]- and [au]-type variants from southern England and the USA. The demographic mix thereafter was such that one vowel quality was not replaced by another during the focusing process. Rather, the generation that first spoke a unified, focused dialect of Canadian English rationalized the situation by redistributing the variants allophonically according to the natural phonetic tendencies described by Chambers. It is also quite possible that reallocation rather than levelling took place because of the salience of the two allophones – which in turn could be due to the degree of phonetic difference between them.

Canadian English shows obvious signs of its mixed British Isles origins in its lexis and grammar: for instance, the word *pinkie* ('little finger'), to give but one example, is generally known in Canada, but not understood in most of England, being confined to Scotland and adjacent areas of England. The construction exemplified in *The dog wants in*, *He wants out* is also found in Scotland but not in most of England. And Scottish and Canadian English share *Did you have lunch yet?* versus English

English *Have you had lunch yet?* (see above). Given that the variety is clearly mixed in this way, then we must expect signs of mixture in the phonology also.

Now, as we saw above, it could be argued that this explanation of the origins of Canadian Raising in dialect mixture seems unlikely to be correct in view of the fact that it does not occur in most of the USA, or in Australia, New Zealand, or South Africa. The very striking fact is, however, that although Canadian Raising does not occur in Britain, it does occur in *nearly every* form of non-creolized, mixed, colonial English outside Australasia and South Africa. It is found not only in Canada but also in at least some of the varieties of English spoken in Bermuda, the Bahamas, Saba, St Helena, Tristan da Cunha, and the Falkland Islands. In St Helena, for example, we find pronunciations such as:

write	[ʋ3ɪt˺]	*prize*	[pʋɒ-ɫ·z]
about	[əbȝʉt]	*down*	[dạ·ᵛn]

while in the English of whites in N. Eleuthera, Bahamas, we find:

right	[ɹ3ɪt]	*side*	[sɑ·ɪd]
house	[h3ʉs]	*down*	[dạʊn]

In the English of Tristan da Cunha, we get realizations such as:

pipe	[pæip]	*ride*	[ɹɑ·ˈd]
out	[œʉt]	*now*	[nạ·ᵘ]

In lower-class white Bermudian we have:

night	[n3ɪt]	*time*	[tɒ:m]
out	[əʉt]	*now*	[nɐ:]

And in the white dialects of the Caribbean island of Saba we have:

out	[əʉt]	*down*	[da·ʉn]

Note the very striking fact that while, in all these dialects, the variants of the diphthongs that occur in voiceless environments have central first elements as in Canadian English, the 'elsewhere' variants are very different from the Canadian [aɪ]- and [au]-type forms. As can be seen, these Atlantic Ocean varieties have longer, backer, and more monophthongal forms. This state of affairs can actually be seen as lending some support to the hypothesis. Tristan English, for example, is a rather younger dialect of English than is Canadian English. This, we can suggest, meant that it was later south-of-England-based developments from [aɪ] and [au], such as the [ɑɪ~ɒɪ] typical of Australasian English, that formed part of the input to the mixture process, rather than the earlier forms found in Canada (see further Trudgill, forthcoming).

Further confirmation of this thesis can be found in the reallocation present in other colonial varieties of English. South African English, for example, shows its mixed origins with the same type of allophonic alternation. Australian English, as we have seen, has a high front vowel [i] as the realization of the /ɪ/ of *bit* (we argued above that this vowel was probably typical of nineteenth-century south-eastern English pronunciation). New Zealand English has /ɪ/ as a central vowel in the region of [ə] – *bit* [bət] (one source for this may well have been the pronunciation of this vowel in Scottish varieties of English, where in most dialects /ɪ/ is a central vowel of the type [ə], [ɜ] or even [ɐ]). Many forms of South African English, on the other hand, realize /ɪ/ both as [i] *and* as [ə], with the two variants being allophonic variants distributed according to phonological environment (see Lanham and Macdonald, 1979). Thus *king* is [kiŋ], while *limb* is [ləm]. Again, reallocation of variants present in the mixture during focusing appears to be a likely explanation for this development.

Conclusion

It now seems reasonable to claim, although we are still very far indeed from being able to explain why colonial varieties are exactly as they are, that a number of the processes involved in dialect mixture are of a widespread or universal type. Most of the mechanisms that we have seen at work in this chapter in the case of transplanted varieties of English, we have also seen at work in the case of other mixed dialects, and *vice versa*. Where mixing takes place, we observe levelling, simplification, reallocation, and the appearance of interdialect forms. These, in turn, can be ascribed to processes that take place during accommodation, which is normally imperfect in long-term dialect contacts, at least in the case of adults, and which depends on degrees of linguistic salience and naturalness, as well as on demographic factors (especially in cases of 'accommodating out'). Accommodation, in its turn, appears to be part of a much wider tendency for human behaviour modification in social interaction.

We do not, of course, know exactly why colonial varieties of English around the world have the characteristics that they do – although we can look, as we have done, at British English dialects and attempt to make sensible explanations – but we do have very strong evidence that they are as they are because of the way in which people behave linguistically in face-to-face interaction. That is, whole new language varieties, many of them eventually spoken by millions of people, grow and develop out of small-scale contacts between individual human beings.

References

Aitken, A. J. (1984) Scottish accents and dialects. In P. Trudgill (ed.) *Language in the British Isles*. London: Cambridge University Press.

Andrésen, B. S. (1968) *Pre-glottalisation in English Standard Pronunciation*. Oslo: Norwegian University Press.

Bähr, D. (1974) *Standard English und seine geographischen Varianten*. Munich: Fink.

Bailey, C. J. (1973) *Variation and Linguistic Theory*. Washington: CAL.

Baker, S. (1966) *The Australian Language*, 2nd ed. Sydney: Currawong.

Bauer, L. (1979) The second Great Vowel Shift? *Journal of the International Phonetic Association* 9, 57–66.

Beal, J. (forthcoming) *The Grammar of Tyneside and Northumbrian English*. London: ESRC.

Bell, A. (1984) Language style as audience design. *Language in Society* 13, 145–204

Bernard, J. (1969) On the uniformity of spoken Australian English. *Orbis* 18, 62–73.

Bhatia, T. (1982) Transplanted South Asian languages: an overview. *Studies in the Linguistic Sciences* 11, 129–34.

Bickerton, D. (1975) *Dynamics of a Creole System*. London: Cambridge University Press.

Bickerton, D. (forthcoming) Explaining 'Language transmission'. Paper given at the Symposium on Language Transmission, CARBS, 1984.

Blair, D. (1975) On the origins of Australian pronunciation. *Working Papers of the Speech and Language Research Centre, Macquarie University*, 17–27.

Bliss, A. (1984) English in the south of Ireland. In P. Trudgill (ed.) *Language in the British Isles*. London: Cambridge University Press.

Bradley, D. (1981) Regional differences in Australian English phonology. *Melbourne University Working Papers in Linguistics* 6, 73–93.

Broselow, E. (1984) An investigation of transfer in second language phonology. *IRAL* 22.

Butters, R. (1980) Unstressed vowels in Appalachian English. *American Speech*, 105–10.

Cappella, J. (1981) Mutual influence in expressive behaviour. *Psychological Bulletin* 89, 101–32.

Chambers, J. (1973) Canadian raising. *Canadian Journal of Linguistics* 18, 113–35.

Chambers, J. (1979) Canadian English. In J. Chambers (ed.) *The Languages of Canada*. Montreal: Didier.

Chambers, J. (1980) Linguistic variation and Chomsky's 'homogeneous speech community'. *Papers from the Fourth Annual Meeting of the Atlantic Provinces Linguistics Association.*

Chambers, J. and Hardwick, M. (1985) Dialect homogeneity and incipient variation. *Sheffield Working Papers in Language and Linguistics* 2.

Chambers, J. and Trudgill, P. (1980) *Dialectology*. London: Cambridge University Press.

Chapman, K. (1962) *Icelandic-Norwegian Linguistic Relationships*. Oslo: Universitetsforlaget.

Cheshire, J. (1982) *Variation in an English Dialect*. London: Cambridge University Press.

Collins, J. (1975) The sources of Australian pronunciation. *Working Papers of the Speech and Language Research Centre, Macquarie University*, 116.

Cooper, V. (1979) Aspects of St. Kitts-Nevis Creole phonology. *Journal of the College of the Virgin Islands* 4, 5–22.

Cooper, V. (1980) Basilectal Creole, decreolisation and autonomous language change in St. Kitts-Nevis. Princeton University: Ph.D. thesis.

Coupland, N. (1984) Accommodation at work. *International Journal of the Sociology of Language* 4–6, 49–70.

Dittman, A. (1962) The relationship between body movements and moods in interviews. *Journal of Consulting Psychology* 26, 480.

Dittman, A. (1972) Developmental factors in conversational behaviour. *Journal of Communication* 22, 404–23.

Dixon, J. (1822) *Narrative of a Voyage to New South Wales and Van Diemen's Land*. Edinburgh: Anderson.

Domingue, N. (1980) Syntactic innovations in Mauritian Bhojpuri. Unpublished manuscript.

Domingue, N. (1981) Internal change in a transplanted language. *Studies in the Linguistic Sciences* 4, 151–9.

Dorian, N. (1973) Grammatical change in a dying dialect. *Language* 49, 413–38.

Edwards, V. K., Trudgill, P. and Weltens, B. (1984) *The Grammar of English Dialect*. London: ESRC.

Ekwall, E. (1960) *English Place Names*, 4th ed. Oxford: Oxford University Press.

Elizaincín, A. (1973) *Algunos aspectos de la sociolingüística del dialecto fronterizo*. Montevideo: Instituto Interamerican del Niño.

Feldstein, S. (1972) Temporal patterns of dialogue. In A. Siegman and D. Pope (eds) *Studies in Dyadic Communication*. New York: Pergamon.

Ferguson, C. (1959) Diglossia. *Word* 15, 325–40.

Francis, W. N. (1967) *The English Language*. London: English Universities Press.

Francis, W. N. (ms.) Field notes for the Survey of English Dialects. University of Leeds.

Gatewood, J. and Rosenwein, R. (1981) Interactional synchrony: genuine or spurious? A critique of recent research. *Journal of Nonverbal Behaviour* 6, 12–29.

Gerstaecker, F. (1853) *Narrative of a Journey round the World*. London: Hurst and Blackett.

Giles, H. (1973) Accent mobility: a model and some data. *Anthropological Linguistics* 15, 87–105.

Giles, H., Taylor, D. and Bourhis, R. (1973) Towards a theory of interpersonal accommodation through speech: some Canadian data. *Language in Society* 2, 177–92.

Giles, H. and Smith, P. (1979) Accommodation theory: optimal levels of convergence. In H. Giles and R. St Clair (eds) *Language and Social Psychology*. Oxford: Basil Blackwell.

Gimson, A. (1980) *An Introduction to the Pronunciation of English*, 3rd ed. London: Edward Arnold.

Gordon, E. (1983) New Zealand English pronunciation: an investigation into some early written records. *Te Reo* 26, 29–42.

Gordon, E. and Deverson, T. (1985) *New Zealand English*. Auckland: Heinemann.

Gregg, R. (1972) The Scotch–Irish dialect boundaries in Ulster. In M. Wakelin (ed.) *Patterns in the Folk Speech of the British Isles*. London: Athlone.

Gregg, R. (1973) The diphthongs əi and ɑi in Scottish, Scotch–Irish and Canadian English. *Canadian Journal of Linguistics* 18, 136–45.

Hammarström, C. (1980) *Australian English: Its Origin and Status*. Hamburg: Buske.

Harris, J. (1984a) English in the north of Ireland. In P. Trudgill (ed.) *Language in the British Isles*. London: Cambridge University Press.

Harris, J. (1984b) Syntactic variation and dialect divergence. *Journal of Linguistics* 20, 303–28.

Haugen, E. (1966) Semicommunication: the language gap in Scandinavia. *Sociological Inquiry* 36, 280–97.

Haugen, E. (1976) *The Scandinavian Languages*. London: Faber.

Henry, P. (1957) *The Anglo-Irish Dialect of North Roscommon*. Dublin: University College.

Hensey, F. (1972) *The Sociolinguistics of the Brazilian–Uruguayan Border*. The Hague: Mouton.

Hensey, F. (1982) Spanish, Portuguese and Fronteiriço: languages in contact in northern Uruguay. *International Journal of the Sociology of Language* 34, 7–24.

Hickey, R. (1984) Coronal segments in Irish English. *Journal of Linguistics* 20, 233–50.

Holm, J. (1986) *Creole Languages*. London: Cambridge University Press.

Hughes, A. and Trudgill, P. (1979) *English Accents and Dialects*. London: Edward Arnold.

Ihalainen, O. (1976) Periphrastic *do* in affirmative sentences in the dialect of East Somerset. *Neuphilologische Mitteilungen* 77, 609–22.

Jaffe, J. and Feldstein, S. (1970) *Rhythms of Dialogue*. New York: Academic.

Jahr, E. H. (1978) Min egen syntaks i intervjuer med kvinner og menn fra Oslo. In K. Gregersen (ed.) *Papers from the Fourth Scandinavian Conference of Linguistics*. Odense: University Press.

Jahr, E. H. (1979) Er det sånn jeg snakker? In J. Kleiven (ed.) *Språk og Samfunn*. Oslo: Pax.

Jenstad, T. E. (1983) *Eit Nytt Sentrumsmål Veks Fram*. Trondheim: Tapir.

Johnston, P. (1984) Variation in the standard Scottish English of Morningside. *English World-Wide* 4, 133–86.

Joos, M. (1942) A phonological dilemma in Canadian English. *Language* 18, 141–4.

Kazazis, K. (1970) The relative importance of parents and peers in first-language acquisition: the case of some Constantinopolitan families in Athens. *General Linguistics* 10, 111–20.

Kendon, A. (1970) Movement coordination in social interaction. *Acta Psychologica* 32, 100–25.

Kerswill, P. (1985) *A Sociolinguistic Study of Rural Immigrants in Bergen, Norway*. Cambridge University, unpublished Ph.D. thesis.

Knowles, G. (1978) The nature of phonological variables in Scouse. In P. Trudgill (ed.) *Sociolinguistic Patterns in British English*. London: Edward Arnold.

Knops, U. (1981) Assimilatie verschijnselen van Vlamingen in Nederland. *Gramma*.

Kökeritz, H. (1932) *The Phonology of the Suffolk Dialect*. Uppsala: Uppsala University.

Kurath, H. (1972) *Studies in Area Linguistics*. Bloomington: Indiana University Press.

Labov, W. (1963) The social motivation of a sound change. *Word* 19, 273–309.

Labov, W. (1966) *The Social Stratification of English in New York City*. Washington: CAL.

Labov, W. (1972) *Sociolinguistic Patterns*. Philadelphia: University of Pennsylvania Press.

Labov, W. (1982) Building on empirical foundations. In W. Lehmann and Y. Malkiel (eds) *Perspectives on Historical Linguistics*. Amsterdam: Philadelphia.

Labov, W. (1983) The three dialects of English. In P. Eckert (ed.) *Quantitative Analyses of Sound Change in Progress*. New York: Academic.

Labov, W. (ms.) On the adequacy of natural language.

Labov, W., Yaeger, M., and Steiner, R. (1972) *A Quantitative Study of Sound Change in Progress*. Philadelphia: U.S. Regional Survey.

Lanham, L. and Macdonald, C. (1979) *The Standard in South African English and its Social History*. Heidelberg: Groos.

Larsen, A. (1907) *Kristiania Bymål*. Kristiania (Oslo).

Larsen, A. (1917) Nabopposition – knot. *Maal og Minne*.

Larsen, A. and Stoltz, G. (1911–12) *Bergens Bymål*. Kristiania (Oslo).

Lass, R. (1984) *Phonology*. London: Cambridge University Press.

LePage, R. and Tabouret-Keller, A. (1985) *Acts of Identity*. London: Cambridge University Press.

Maclaran, R. (1976) The variable (ʌ): a relic form with social correlates. *Belfast Working Papers in Language and Linguistics* 1, 45–68.

Martinet, A. (1955) *Economie des Changements Phonétiques*. Berne: Francke.

Matias, M. (1984) *Bilinguismo e Níveis Sociolinguísticos numa Região Luso-Espanhola*. Coimbra: University of Coimbra.

Miller, S. (1978) Camp transport before the machine age. *The Falklands Island Journal*.

Milroy, J. (1978) Lexical alternation and diffusion in vernacular speech. *Belfast Working Papers in Language and Linguistics* 3, 100–14.

Milroy, J. (1981) *Regional Accents of English: Belfast*. Belfast: Blackstaff.

Milroy, J. (1982) Probing under the tip of the iceberg: phonological 'normalisation' and the shape of speech communities. In S. Romaine (ed.) *Sociolinguistic Variation in Speech Communities*. London: Edward Arnold.

Milroy, J. (1983) On the sociolinguistic history of /h/-dropping in English. In M. Davenport et al. (eds) *Proceedings of the Second International Conference on Historical Linguistics*. Odense: Odense University.

Milroy, J. and Milroy, L. (1978) Belfast: change and variation in an urban vernacular. In P. Trudgill (ed.) *Sociolinguistic Patterns in British English*. London: Edward Arnold.

Milroy, J. and Milroy, L. (1985) Linguistic change, social network and speaker innovation. *Journal of Linguistics* 21.

Milroy, L. (1980) *Language and Social Networks*. Oxford: Basil Blackwell.

Milroy, L. (1984) Comprehension and context: successful communication and communication breakdown. In P. Trudgill (ed.) *Applied Sociolinguistics*. London: Academic.

Miranda, R. (ms.) On the origins of Fiji Hindi.

Moag, R. (1977) *Fiji Hindi*. Canberra: Australian National University Press.

Mohan, P. (1978) Trinidad Bhojpuri. University of Michigan: Ph.D. thesis.

Mühlhäusler, P. (1977) *Pidginisation and Simplification of Language*. Canberra: Pacific Linguistics.

Newbrook, M. (1982) Scot or Scouser?: an anomalous informant in outer Merseyside. *English World-Wide* 3, 77–86.

Nordenstam, K. (1979) *Svenskan i Norge*. Gothenberg: University Press.

Ølmheim, P. (1983) *Sa Sogningen til Fjordingen*. Bergen: Sogn Mållag, Firda Mållag.

Omdal, H. (1976) Høyanger har skiftet talemål. *Bergens Tidende*, 13 April.

Omdal, H. (1977) Høyangermålet – en ny dialekt. *Språklig Samling* 1.

Ó Muirithe, D. (1977) *The English Language in Ireland*. Dublin: Mercier.

Orton, H. et al. (1962–71) *Survey of English Dialects*, introduction and four volumes. Leeds: E. J. Arnold.

Orton et al. (1978) *The Linguistic Atlas of England*. London: Croom Helm.

Patterson, M. (1973) Compensation of nonverbal immediary behaviours: a review. *Sociometry* 237–52.

Patterson, M. (1983) *Nonverbal Behaviour*. New York: Springer.

Payne, A. (1976) The Acquisition of the Phonological System of a Second Dialect. Unpublished thesis. University of Pennsylvania.

Payne, A. (1980) Factors controlling the acquisition of the Philadelphia dialect by out-of-state children. In W. Labov (ed.) *Locating Language in Time and Space*. New York: Academic.

Pringle, I. (1981) The Gaelic substratum in the English of Glengarry County. *Canadian Journal of Linguistics* 26, 113–17.

Quirk, R., Greenbaum, S., Leech, G, and Svartvik, J. (1972) *A Grammar of Contemporary English*. London: Longmans.

Rekdal, O. (1971) *Modifisert Dialekt*. Unpublished thesis. Oslo University.

Robinson, D. (1971) *Son of Bristle*. Bristol: Abson.

Rogers, I. (1981) The influence of Australian English intonation on the speech of two British children. *Working Papers of the Speech and Language Research Centre, Macquarie University* 3, 25–42.

Rona, J. (1963) La frontera lingüistica entre el portugués y el español en el norte del Uruguay. *Veritas* 2, 201–20.

Rona, J. (1965) *El Dialecto 'Fronterizo' de Norte del Uruguay*. Montevideo: Lonaldi.

Selinker, L. (1972) Interlanguage. *IRAL* 10, 209–31.

Shockey, L. (ms.) A phonological change in Eastern Transatlantic English.

Shopen, T. (ms.) Research on the variable (ng) in Canberra, Australia.

Shukla, S. (1981) *Bhojpuri Grammar*. Washington: Georgetown University.

Spencer, N. (1975) Singular *y'all*. *American Speech*.

Steinsholt, A. (1962) *Målbryting i Hedrum*. Oslo: Universitetsforlaget.

Story, G., Kirwin, W, and Widdowson, J. (1982) *Dictionary of Newfoundland English*. Toronto: Amnesty Press.

Strang, B. (1970) *A History of English*. London: Methuen.

Strange, I. (1973) Introduction of stock to the Falkland Islands. *The Falkland Islands Journal*.

Thelander, M. (1979) *Språkliga Variationsmodeller Tillämpade på Nutida Burträsktal*. Uppsala: Uppsala University.

Timberlake, A. (1977) Reanalysis and actualisation in syntactic change. In C. Li (ed.) *Mechanisms of Syntactic Change*. Austin: University of Texas.

Trudgill, P. (1974) *The Social Differentiation of English in Norwich*. London: Cambridge University Press.

Trudgill, P. (1982) Linguistic accommodation: sociolinguistic observations on a sociopsychological theory. In T. Fretheim and L. Hellan (eds) *Sixth Scandinavian Conference of Linguistics*. Trondheim: Tapir.

Trudgill, P. (1983) *On Dialect*. Oxford: Basil Blackwell.

Trudgill, P. (forthcoming) *Language in Isolation*.

Trudgill, P. and Hannah, J. (1982) *International English: a Guide to Varieties of Standard English*. London: Edward Arnold.

Turner, G. (1966) *The English Language in Australia and New Zealand*. London: Longmans.

Venås, K. (1982) *Mål og Miljø*. Oslo: Novus.

Viereck, W. (1980) The dialectal structure of British English: Lowman's evidence. *English World-Wide* 1, 25–44.

Vigeland, B. (1981) *Dialekter i Norge*. Oslo: Universitetsforlaget.

Wang, W. (1969) Competing changes as a cause of residue. *Language* 45, 9–25.

Weinreich, U. (1953) *Languages in Contact*. New York: Linguistic Circle.

Wells, J. (1982) *Accents of English*, three volumes. London: Cambridge University Press.

Weltens, B. (ms.) Nonstandard periphrastic *do* in the dialects of south-west Britain.

Index